TEEN CHALLENGES

UNPLANNED PREGNANCIES

by Alexis Burling

CONTENT CONSULTANT
Laura Widman, PhD
Associate Professor of Psychology
North Carolina State University

Essential Library

An Imprint of Abdo Publishing | abdobooks.com

ABDOBOOKS.COM

Published by Abdo Publishing, a division of ABDO, PO Box 398166, Minneapolis, Minnesota 55439. Copyright © 2022 by Abdo Consulting Group, Inc. International copyrights reserved in all countries. No part of this book may be reproduced in any form without written permission from the publisher. Essential Library™ is a trademark and logo of Abdo Publishing.

Printed in the United States of America, North Mankato, Minnesota.
102021
012022

Cover Photo: VG Stock Studio/Shutterstock Images
Interior Photos: Shutterstock Images, 4, 14–15, 50, 72; iStockphoto, 7, 12, 40–41, 54, 62, 68, 88–89; Krakenimages.com/Shutterstock Images, 16; Olga Bolbot/Shutterstock Images, 20; Gpoint Studio/iStockphoto, 24; People Images/iStockphoto, 26–27; Antonio Guillem/iStockphoto, 28; Postmodern Studio/Shutterstock Images, 30; Purple Anvil/Shutterstock Images, 33; Andrey Popov/Shutterstock Images, 38–39; SDI Productions/iStockphoto, 44; Red Line Editorial, 46; Caroline Brehman/CQ Roll Call/AP Images, 56; Anita Patterson Peppers/Shutterstock Images, 66; Monkey Business Images/iStockphoto, 74–75; Rostislav Sedlacek/iStockphoto, 80; Fat Camera/iStockphoto, 84–85; Rawpixel/iStockphoto, 87; New Africa/Shutterstock Images, 90; ErsinTekkol/Shutterstock Images, 92; Global Stock/iStockphoto, 95; Image Source/Getty Images, 99

Editor: Alyssa Krekelberg
Series Designer: Colleen McLaren

LIBRARY OF CONGRESS CONTROL NUMBER: 2021941235

PUBLISHER'S CATALOGING-IN-PUBLICATION DATA

Names: Burling, Alexis, author.

Title: Unplanned pregnancies / by Alexis Burling

Description: Minneapolis, Minnesota : Abdo Publishing, 2022 | Series: Teen challenges | Includes online resources and index.

Identifiers: ISBN 9781532196317 (lib. bdg.) | ISBN 9781098218126 (ebook)

Subjects: LCSH: Unplanned pregnancy--Juvenile literature. | Teenage pregnancy--Juvenile literature. | Youth--Sexual behavior--Juvenile literature. | Teenage mothers--Juvenile literature. | Teenage fathers--Juvenile literature.

Classification: DDC 306.874--dc23

CONTENTS

CHAPTER ONE
A LIFE-CHANGING
MOMENT. 04

CHAPTER TWO
GETTING PREGNANT AND
THE SYMPTOMS. 16

CHAPTER THREE
BIRTH CONTROL OPTIONS. . 28

CHAPTER FOUR
TEEN PREGNANCY ON
THE DECLINE. 44

CHAPTER FIVE
PUBLIC POLICY
AND DEMOGRAPHICS 56

CHAPTER SIX
MAKING THE CHOICE 68

CHAPTER SEVEN
THE COST OF
PREGNANCY 80

CHAPTER EIGHT
EFFECTS ON
DAILY LIFE 90

ESSENTIAL FACTS. 100
GLOSSARY 102
ADDITIONAL RESOURCES. 104
SOURCE NOTES 106
INDEX 110
ABOUT THE AUTHOR. 112
ABOUT THE CONSULTANT 112

People's emotions can vary when they discover they're pregnant. Some might be overjoyed, while others are stressed.

CHAPTER ONE

A LIFE-CHANGING MOMENT

More than a week had passed since she had slept with Jeremy for the first time, and 16-year-old Leah was an emotional wreck. Over the last few days she had become very withdrawn. She dusted and vacuumed the house, and she put all her clothes neatly away in the closet. She even scrubbed the tub and toilet in the bathroom she shared with her older sister, Stacey. Her family definitely suspected something was up. She told them she was having friend issues so they wouldn't worry about her too much.

But Leah couldn't stop going over what had happened that night, no matter how many things she cleaned to try to distract herself. The truth was that she and Jeremy had done everything "right." Well, almost. They had waited six months after they first got together before having sex. They had talked about having sex endlessly before the big night to make sure each of them was comfortable and interested. But the one thing they didn't do was use

> "ANY GIRL WHO HAS UNPROTECTED VAGINAL INTERCOURSE RUNS THE RISK OF BECOMING PREGNANT, WHETHER IT'S HER FIRST TIME HAVING SEX OR THE 100TH TIME. IT'S EVEN POSSIBLE TO BECOME PREGNANT BEFORE EVER HAVING A PERIOD."[1]
>
> —AMY, AN EXPERT AT PLANNED PARENTHOOD

EMERGENCY CONTRACEPTION

Some situations may lead people to use emergency contraception. If the condom breaks, if it was unprotected sex, if the original birth control method wasn't used correctly, or if there's another reason to suspect pregnancy, girls can take a fast-acting pill that will prevent a pregnancy from taking place. It works by temporarily stopping the ovary from releasing an egg. But it must be taken within five days after having sex to be as effective as possible.

a condom. In all their nervousness, Jeremy had forgotten the box in his locker at school. They decided to have sex anyway, and Jeremy would just pull out. Leah wasn't on any form of birth control, but they didn't think it would be a problem.

The actual having sex part was sort of goofy and awkward, especially because Jeremy didn't exactly pull out in time. But beyond that, the whole night was fine. Leah brought up the possibility of taking the morning-after pill, but Jeremy said her chances of getting pregnant on the first time were super low. Besides, her period was supposed to hit in

It's important for people to have a partner that they can trust.

a week, so they decided to wait and see what happened. In the meantime, Leah said she'd go out and get a pack of condoms so they'd be prepared the next time.

TAKING THE TEST

A week later, Leah still hadn't gotten her period even though she had cramps and her mood was all over the place. The next couple weeks passed, and Leah kept hoping for it to happen, but her period never came. Whether she wanted to or not, it was time to go to the drug store. At this point she was tired of obsessing about whether her period had arrived every time she went to the bathroom. She just wanted to know what was going on.

FALSE POSITIVES

Home pregnancy tests are pretty accurate. But there are a few reasons why a test can produce a false positive result. Pregnancy tests work by detecting a hormone called human chorionic gonadotropin (HCG) in a woman's urine. One reason a pregnancy test might produce a false positive result is if HCG is present for another reason. This usually only happens if the woman is taking a drug that contains HCG, such as one used to treat infertility.

Another reason a pregnancy test can fail is if the user doesn't follow directions properly. Most tests instruct women to read the result within four or five minutes of taking the test. If they wait too long to read the results, some of the urine might evaporate. This could produce a line on the stick that looks like a positive result.

For the past few days, Jeremy had been pretty supportive. He sent her a bunch of texts asking her whether she was all right and whether there was anything he could do. But though he offered to go to the drug store with her, Leah told him it was something she needed to do on her own. At the last minute, she ended up telling Stacey a short version of what was going on, just so she'd have some company in case her fears were realized. Ever the level-headed older sister, Stacey didn't ask too many questions. She just listened and told

Leah she'd be there for whatever Leah needed. Stacey also promised not to tell their parents—at least not yet.

When they got home from the drug store, the sisters went directly into the bathroom. Leah opened the box, read the instructions, took a deep breath, and peed on the stick. Then they waited. After several minutes, Leah asked her sister to look at the stick because she wasn't yet ready to do so. With an unreadable expression, Stacey suggested Leah take the other test they bought just to be sure. Leah opened the second box, read the instructions, took another deep breath, and peed into a cup. After dunking the new stick into the cup, she put it on the counter and waited. Finally, Stacey looked at the second stick and handed both to her sister. Leah was pregnant.

"IF ANYTHING DOESN'T MAKE SENSE, GO SEE A DOCTOR. IF YOU ARE HAVING BLEEDING BUT THE PREGNANCY TEST IS POSITIVE, IF YOU ARE VERY LATE ON YOUR PERIOD BUT DO NOT HAVE A POSITIVE PREGNANCY TEST, GO SEE YOUR DOCTOR."[2]

—DR. STEPHANIE ROMERO, ASSISTANT PROFESSOR AT THE UNIVERSITY OF SOUTH FLORIDA MORSANI COLLEGE OF MEDICINE

REVIEWING THE OPTIONS

The next morning, Leah was exhausted. She spent half the night sobbing and the other half screaming into her pillow. When she had gone to Jeremy's to tell him the news, he had freaked out and told her he needed some solo time to think. Leah felt more alone than she ever had in her life.

Thankfully, Stacey was on top of the situation. She had kept a respectful distance the night before, but by the next afternoon she had made an appointment for Leah at the local Planned Parenthood. Though Leah stayed home from school and begged to stay in her pajamas all day, Stacey dragged her to the office.

The doctor who came to meet them was exceptionally kind. After doing another pregnancy test and confirming the positive result, she explained Leah's options. Leah could either have the

TALKING TO TRUSTED ADULTS

It's a good idea to talk to a parent or guardian if there's a pregnancy scare. But some caregiver-child relationships might be strained for many reasons. Therefore, it's important to discuss the complicated nature of the caregiver-child relationship with the doctor during the appointment. Most medical providers are required by law to keep their patients' health records confidential. But some of these laws vary from state to state, especially if a teenager is involved.

baby and choose to parent, have the baby and place the child up for adoption, or have an abortion. She handed Leah a stack of pamphlets to take home so she could read about prenatal appointments and other pregnancy logistics.

Stacey thanked the doctor and gave Leah a giant hug as they walked out of the building. Stacey told her sister that the next few days would be some of the toughest she'd ever experience in her life. But no matter what, Stacey said she would be there to support her. As for Leah, she had some serious thinking to do and a decision to make. It would be scary and emotionally draining. But she would get through it.

PRENATAL APPOINTMENT

People who are expecting a baby need to go to prenatal appointments for the full length of their pregnancy. The first one is especially important. During this visit, the obstetrician does a full physical exam. She reviews the patient's full medical history and family background. She also might do a fetal ultrasound. An ultrasound is also known as a sonogram. It is an imaging technique that uses sound waves to produce images of a fetus in the uterus. It helps doctors monitor a baby's growth and development during a pregnancy.

TEEN PREGNANCY IN THE UNITED STATES

Leah's experiences might sound overwhelming, but they are not uncommon. They represent the challenges

People might withdraw from friends or family if they feel anxious or depressed about a pregnancy.

that thousands of teens in the United States encounter each year when faced with an unplanned pregnancy. In fact, the teen birth rate in the United States is higher than that of many other developed countries, including Canada and the United Kingdom. According to the

Centers for Disease Control and Prevention (CDC), in 2018 a total of 179,871 babies were born to girls aged 15 to 19 in the United States.[3] The girls represented all races, were from every state, and were from every type of socioeconomic background.

Dealing with an unplanned pregnancy is never easy. It affects all aspects of daily life. It interferes with schoolwork, social relationships, family life, college or employment prospects, and other plans for the future. It also impacts the physical and mental health of these teens and their loved ones.

Yet despite these challenges, the situation is not insurmountable. The first step is trying to prevent an unplanned pregnancy from occurring whenever possible. That means delaying sexual activity until the teen is ready and learning about every type of birth control available before deciding to have sex. Several of the most common birth control options include condoms, patches, vaginal rings, intrauterine devices (IUDs), implants, and shots. Teens also need to understand exactly how a pregnancy occurs, from the first moment of genital contact, to the fertilization of an egg by a sperm, to the egg's implantation on the uterine wall.

If a girl suspects she might be pregnant, knowing the symptoms of pregnancy and which pregnancy tests to take—including how and when to take them—is key. If the test comes back positive, reviewing next-step options with a counselor, medical professional, or trusted adult is also crucial so she can decide what's best for her and everyone else involved. No matter what the outcome—whether it's parenting, adoption, or abortion—becoming familiar with pregnancy resources and addressing an unplanned pregnancy head-on is essential to ensuring the girl's mental, physical, and emotional health.

Opening up to a trusted adult can help teens feel less isolated.

Women develop their baby bump at different times, but often people start showing between 12 and 16 weeks.

CHAPTER TWO

GETTING PREGNANT AND THE SYMPTOMS

For some women, finding out they're pregnant is a wonderful experience. But for others—especially teens who are still in high school, living at home, or are just starting to have sex—pregnancy can come as an unwanted surprise. Possible reactions might include anger, frustration, guilt, or denial. Shock, fear, anxiety, or depression are also common.

Whether it's planned or not, pregnancy affects everyone involved—both the girl and her partner, and potentially the couple's parents, grandparents, or caregivers. It impacts not only the immediate future, but also long-term goals. For example, some girls who get pregnant at 16 might have to give up their dreams of going to their first-choice college or embarking on an exciting career.

But before jumping from unprotected sex or a broken condom to "I'm pregnant, and my life as I know it is over," it's important to understand the science behind how a woman becomes pregnant. It's also a good idea to become familiar with the early signs of pregnancy and how to tell for sure whether a pregnancy scare is, in fact, a reality.

HOW PREGNANCIES OCCUR

In very basic terms, pregnancy becomes possible after a person hits puberty. The reproductive anatomy goes through several life-altering changes. For boys, two ball-like glands called testicles underneath the penis start producing sperm and continue to do so for the rest of their lives. The sperm is stored in the epididymis, a tube that connects to each testicle, where they continue to develop and grow. When a boy becomes aroused, the sperm travels up through another set of tubes called the vas deferens and into the ejaculatory duct. There, they wait to be released by the penis through muscle contractions. During ejaculation, the prostate gland and seminal vesicles release a milky substance called semen, which contains millions of sperm.

"GOING THROUGH A TEEN PREGNANCY IS PROBABLY NOT GOING TO BE EASY. HOWEVER, IT IS DEFINITELY POSSIBLE. YOUNG WOMEN . . . PUSH THROUGH THE TRIALS OF TEEN PREGNANCY EVERY DAY."[1]

—AMERICAN PREGNANCY ASSOCIATION

Girls are born with thousands of tiny eggs that live inside the ovaries, which are twin organs in the lower abdomen. When a girl reaches puberty, she starts going through a process called the menstrual cycle, which gives her body the chance to create a baby. Approximately every month, her ovaries release a mature egg into the fallopian tubes, where it waits for 24 hours to be fertilized by a single sperm. This is called ovulation. At the same time, the lining of the uterus thickens in preparation for conception, or the fertilization of the egg. If none occurs, the uterine lining and blood are discarded from her vagina during menstruation.

MYTHS AND FACTS OF PREGNANCY

Understanding what takes place when a girl becomes pregnant can prevent it from happening in the first place. There are common misconceptions about pregnancy. One myth is that a girl can't get pregnant the first time she has sex. But any time a girl has vaginal sex and sperm are involved, she can become pregnant—even the first time. Another myth is that a girl can't get pregnant during her period. A girl can get pregnant if ovulation happens before her period stops or if it occurs within a few days after her period is over. Sperm can survive in the female's reproductive system for up to five days. But an egg needs to be fertilized within 12 to 24 hours in order for a pregnancy to occur. A third myth is that a girl can't get pregnant if she doesn't have her period. In fact, although it's uncommon, girls can get pregnant even if they haven't started menstruating yet.

REPRODUCTIVE SYSTEMS

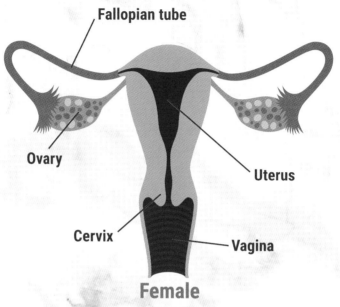

Female

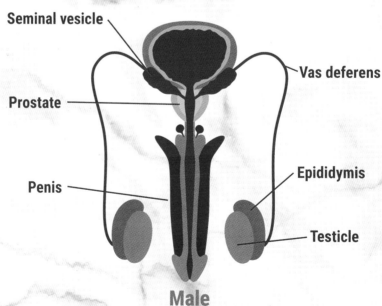

Male

If semen is released by the penis into the vagina during sex and sperm comes into contact with an egg, pregnancy is possible. Once fertilization occurs, the fertilized egg starts dividing into tiny cells. This bundle of cells moves through the fallopian tube toward the uterus. If it attaches itself to the uterine wall to absorb nutrients, the woman is pregnant. Within three weeks, the divided cells grow into clumps, which means the embryo's first nerve cells have started to form. At the end of week eight, most of the brain,

THE GROWTH STAGES OF PREGNANCY

There are different growth stages of fetal development, which usually lasts between 37 and 40 weeks. In the first phase called the germinal stage, the egg is fertilized by the sperm to form a zygote. The zygote then divides into tiny clumps of cells and travels down the fallopian tube toward the uterus. Once implanted on the uterine wall, the pregnancy enters the embryonic stage. During these eight weeks, structures such as the bones, heart, brain, and internal organs are formed.

At the eighth week, the fetal stage begins, and the embryo becomes a fetus. During the last 29 weeks of the pregnancy, the organs continue to grow until the baby is ready to be born. For example, teeth appear during weeks nine through 12. Finger and toenails, eyelashes, and eyebrows appear during weeks 16 through 20. By week 36, the fetus should be about 19 to 21 inches (48 to 53 cm) long. Some babies are born earlier or later than 37 weeks, depending on the circumstances.

nerves, heart, stomach, intestines, muscles, and skin have begun to develop.

SYMPTOMS

The first sign of pregnancy is a missed period. But knowing the difference between a missed period and one that is just a little late can be tricky for many reasons. Some girls have a naturally irregular menstrual cycle. Their period doesn't arrive at the same time every month, so it can be difficult to know whether it's more than a week late. Others have a regular cycle but aren't familiar with how to keep track of it. Sometimes they don't know how to tell when their period is late. Still others may have an irregular cycle because of excessive exercising, dieting, low body fat, or an eating disorder such as anorexia. Just like every girl's personality is different, so is her experience with menstruation, ovulation, and pregnancy.

However, there are some common early physical and emotional signs of pregnancy. Moodiness and excessive bloating are common due to hormonal changes in the body. The breasts can become swollen, causing a tingling sensation or a sensitivity to touch. They may feel heavier, and the area around the nipples, called the areola, might darken.

Many people report feeling nauseous, with or without vomiting, at all hours of the day. Also called morning sickness, this wooziness usually begins a month into the pregnancy. It can be triggered by strong smells, spicy foods, or even nothing at all. Other common symptoms include extreme fatigue, increased urination, nasal congestion, and the slowing down of the digestive system, which can lead to constipation.

Two symptoms that can be deceptive are cramping and light bleeding, also called spotting. The light bleeding that happens at the start of pregnancy is a product of the egg's implantation onto the uterine wall. These abdominal pains resemble menstrual cramps but are much lighter. Still, some girls mistake them for the start of their period. One of

WHAT IS AN IRREGULAR MENSTRUAL CYCLE?

The menstrual cycle is counted from the first day of one period to the first day of the next. It's not the same for every girl. Bleeding might occur from every 21 days to every 35 days. It can last anywhere from two to seven days. For teens who have just started their periods, long cycles are common. They shorten and become more regular as girls age.

Some girls have irregular cycles. This can happen for many reasons, including excessive exercising or weight loss, premature ovarian failure, pelvic inflammatory disease, uterine fibroids, hormonal changes, genetics, and pregnancy. The best way to keep track of a menstrual cycle is to make note of the period's end date, the type of blood flow, and any abnormal bleeding. Ovulation typically happens about 14 days before bleeding starts.

Cramping during pregnancy is a sign that the uterus is expanding.

the ways to tell that a pregnancy has occurred is that a white, milky substance from the vagina accompanies the light bleeding. This discharge is caused by an increased growth of cells along the vagina's walls.

PREGNANCY TESTS

The most definitive way for a girl to tell whether she's pregnant is by taking a pregnancy test. Doctors recommend waiting at least a week until after a missed period before doing so. If her period is irregular, she should wait one to two weeks until after having sex to get an accurate result. Girls can visit a school nurse, health clinic, medical office, or Planned Parenthood and have them do either a blood or urine test. Another option is to use an over-the-counter (OTC) method at home that only tests the urine.

There are many types of OTC pregnancy tests available. They can be purchased at a pharmacy, a dollar store, some grocery stores, or even online. Most cost anywhere from one dollar to more than $20. They typically test the urine for human chorionic gonadotropin (HCG). This hormone is released in the body when a fertilized egg attaches to the uterine lining. It's typically only present in pregnant women.

EARLY RESPONSE RESULTS

Most doctors recommend waiting to take a pregnancy test until after a missed period to prevent any potential for inaccurate results. But there are tests on the market that can detect a pregnancy before the next monthly menstrual cycle begins. According to Dr. Mary Jane Minkin, clinical professor of obstetrics, gynecology, and reproductive sciences at Yale School of Medicine, some tests can give positive results six days before a girl's period is scheduled to begin.

Some tests instruct the woman to pee into a cup and then insert a testing stick into the cup. For others, the test taker just pees directly onto the stick. The way the results are communicated varies. Usually there's a visible sign, such as a change in the stick's color, a line on a screen, a plus or minus symbol, or the words *pregnant* or *not pregnant*. According to Cleveland Clinic, most tests are very accurate when taken after a missed period. But if taken too early, such as right after having sex or less than a week before a missed period, results could be inaccurate.

People can take multiple at-home tests to be extra sure of the results.

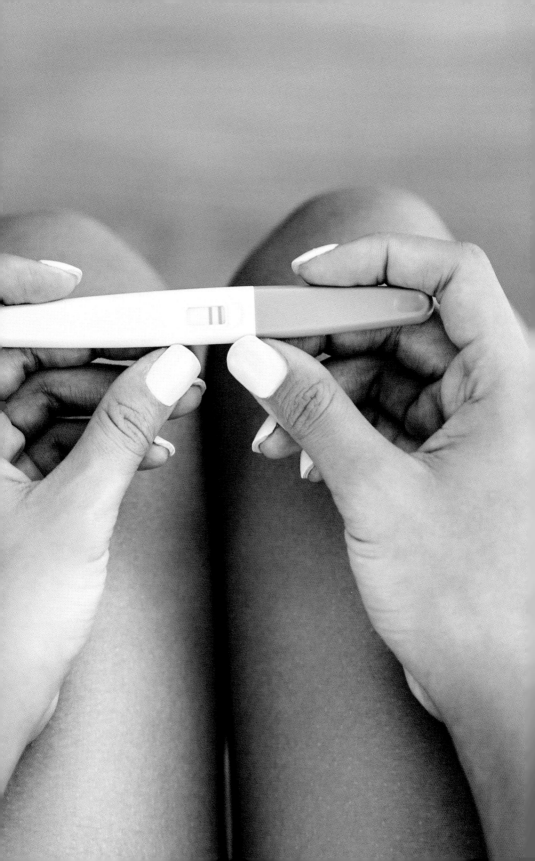

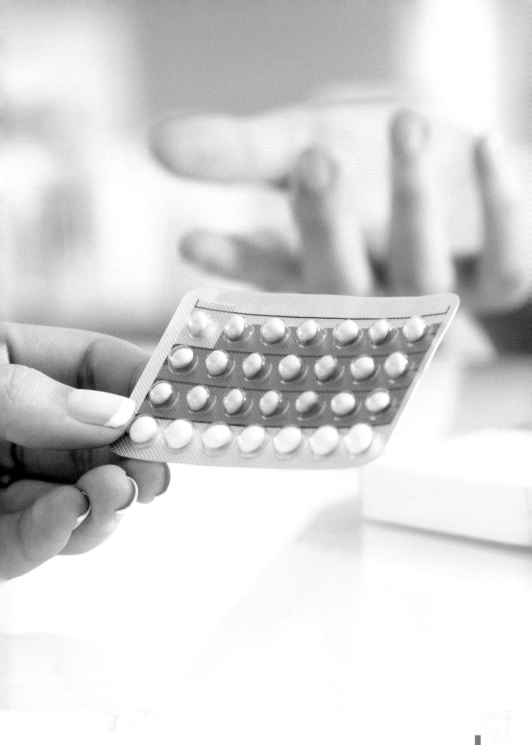

Birth control pills can be prescribed by a doctor or nurse.

CHAPTER THREE

BIRTH CONTROL OPTIONS

Thinking about whether to have sex and when is a complicated decision. There are many factors to consider, including timing, location, and finding the right partner. But health-care providers agree that the one thing that should never be left up to chance is birth control. According to Planned Parenthood, people who have vaginal sex without using any type of birth control have an 85 percent chance of getting pregnant within a year.[1]

There are many types of birth control to choose from, each with different benefits and side effects. Some, such as contraceptive pills, patches, shots, and rings, work by releasing various types of synthetic hormones that prevent sperm from reaching and fertilizing an egg. They do so by either stopping the body from naturally ovulating, changing the uterine lining, thickening the cervical mucus, or a combination of all three. The hormones can also help ease menstrual cramps and clear up acne.

Others, such as the condom and cervical cap, are barrier methods that physically block sperm from getting to the egg. Condoms are the only form of birth control that can protect against sexually transmitted

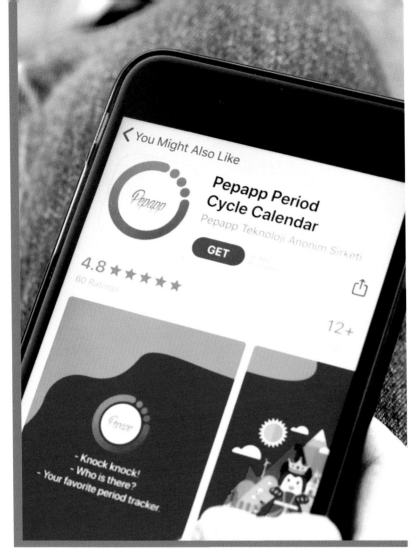

Apps can help women track their cycle. That way, they'll know when to expect their next period.

infections (STIs), so many people use them in addition to another type of method to prevent pregnancy.

People can also use the pull-out method, in which the boy pulls out before he ejaculates, though that is not as effective as other types of birth control. Women can keep track of their ovulation cycles and only have sex on days when they are least fertile. The only sure way to prevent pregnancy, however, is abstinence.

No matter the situation, some forms of birth control are more reliable than others. Birth control's effectiveness depends on how accurately and consistently it is used. For example, a woman who only wears her patch some of the time might be more susceptible to getting pregnant compared with someone who wears it properly. A boy who only sometimes uses a condom might wind up becoming a father earlier than he planned. In addition, sometimes people are physically unable to use certain methods of birth control

THE RHYTHM METHOD: PROS & CONS

The rhythm method, also called the calendar method, is often used by women who want to have a baby. They track their menstrual history in order to predict when they might ovulate and be most likely to conceive. It can also be used to help prevent pregnancy. If a woman knows she's most likely to ovulate on certain days, she can avoid having unprotected sex on those days.

This type of birth control is inexpensive and safe. But there are many drawbacks and risks involved with using it—especially for teens. Some women, particularly those with irregular cycles, might find that keeping an account of their menstrual cycle is time-consuming and confusing. Medications, stress, and illness can also interfere with or disrupt the timing of ovulation. According to the Mayo Clinic, about one-fourth of women who use the rhythm method for birth control become pregnant in the first year of using this option.

because of health risks they might pose, such as a higher susceptibility to blood clots. A woman's body might also react negatively to synthetic hormones, causing mood swings, weight gain, or acne. In this case, there are many other birth control options to choose from.

BARRIER METHODS

A barrier method is a type of birth control that blocks sperm from reaching the egg by physically stopping them from entering the vagina. It must be worn or used every time during sex to help prevent a pregnancy. The most popular choice is the external condom. Made of latex, plastic, or lambskin, it covers the penis during sex and collects semen. According to Planned Parenthood, it prevents pregnancy 98 percent of the time when it's used correctly and consistently.[2] The plastic and latex versions also protect users against STIs. Condoms are available in places such as grocery stores, pharmacies, dollar stores, gas stations, health clinics, and online.

There is also an internal condom, often referred to as a female condom, that is inserted into the vagina or anus and is made out of plastic rather than latex. It's slightly less effective at preventing pregnancy at a 95 percent rate and is not as widely available.[3] Overall, condoms have no side effects, though a small number of people do have a latex allergy.

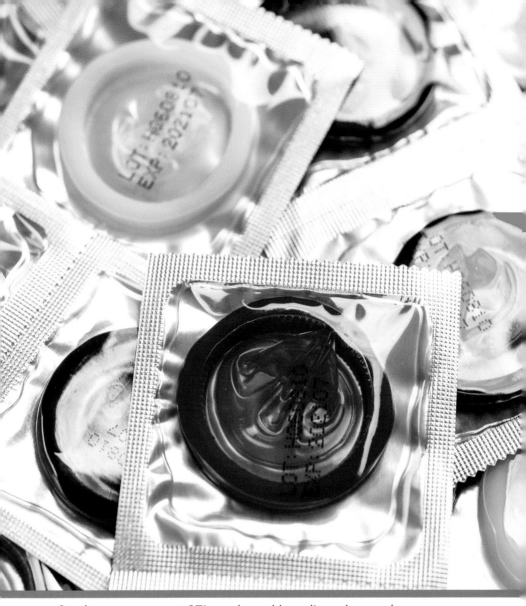

Condoms can prevent STIs such as chlamydia and gonorrhea.

Diaphragms and cervical caps are small, bendable cups that are filled with spermicide or foam and inserted into the vagina before sex. They sit against the cervix. If used perfectly, diaphragms are 94 percent effective at preventing pregnancy.[4] Cervical caps are 86 percent

WHAT IS SPERMICIDE?

Spermicide is a type of cream, gel, film, or foam that is used to prevent pregnancy. It is inserted deep into the vagina prior to sex and works by stopping the sperm from reaching the cervix. It contains nonoxynol-9, a chemical ingredient that cripples the sperm so they can't swim well enough to reach the egg. Spermicide is 71 percent effective if used correctly every time during sex. It costs between five dollars and $15 for a tube. There's no prescription required.

Spermicide can be used on its own. But most doctors agree that it's best used in combination with other methods, such as a condom or diaphragm. About 28 out of 100 people who use just spermicide become pregnant every year, according to Planned Parenthood.[6]

effective for users who have never given birth and 71 percent effective for users who have given birth.[5] Neither protects against STIs. Diaphragms and cervical caps are available at pharmacies or drugstores, but they require a prescription. They also come in different sizes, so they need to be fitted to the body by a health-care provider. Some women complain of getting a urinary tract infection from using them.

The sponge is a device that looks and acts just like its name. It's made of squishy plastic and is inserted into the vagina before sex. It covers the cervix, blocks the entrance to the uterus, and releases spermicide to prevent pregnancy. It's about 90 percent effective when used properly by women who have never given birth before and 80 percent for those who have.[7] When using a sponge, a woman can have sex as many times as she wants within a 24-hour period. But she must leave the sponge in for six hours after the last time she had sex before discarding it. Many women claim that while convenient, this method is messy and can't be used during menstruation.

BIRTH CONTROL PILLS

The birth control pill is another popular option for preventing pregnancy because it is 99 percent effective if used correctly. Depending on the user's health insurance, birth control pills can cost anywhere

BIRTH CONTROL PILLS: PROS AND CONS

There are many different types of birth control pills. Some packs contain a week of hormone-free pills to take during the time the hormone-filled pill isn't meant to be taken, just to reinforce the habit of taking one daily. Others don't. Some need to be taken continuously in order to prevent the body from menstruating. Still others are effective immediately if they're taken within five days of a period. Like many hormonal methods, they can lessen cramps, clear up acne, and lighten periods.

But there are some drawbacks to taking birth control pills. A few brands have a higher level of hormones than others, making them harder for some women's bodies to process. It's also possible to experience spotting between periods, headaches, weight gain, mood swings, a reduction in sex drive, or nausea. Women should talk to a doctor to find the right fit.

from zero dollars to $50 for a month's supply.[8] Medical professionals can provide a prescription, and the pills can be picked up at a pharmacy or sometimes delivered through mail.

There are two types of birth control pills. Combination pills contain two hormones: estrogen and progestin. These hormones are similar to the kinds naturally made by the body. They work by preventing ovulation. They also thicken the cervix's mucus, which blocks sperm from reaching an egg. For most pill packs, one pill must be taken every day at the same time each day for three weeks, then one week off, in order to be effective. The second type are progestin-only pills. They have to be taken at the same time every day, every week of the month, in order to work. If there are any errors in taking these pills, the risk of pregnancy increases.

BIRTH CONTROL PATCHES

The patch is a prescription-based method of birth control. It's a bandage-type device that women wear on their arm, stomach, back, or behind. It releases estrogen and progestin into the body through the skin.

The schedule for wearing it is similar to certain types of birth control pills: three weeks on and one week off. One patch should be used per week. If used correctly, the patch is 99 percent effective. One pack of three patches can cost anywhere from zero dollars to $150, depending on insurance.[9]

VAGINAL RINGS

Like the diaphragm or sponge, the vaginal ring is a flexible device that women place inside their vaginas to prevent pregnancy. Also called the NuvaRing, it contains estrogen and progestin. The device works by releasing these hormones into the vaginal lining. This stops ovulation and thickens cervical mucus.

Users wear one for a certain amount of time—either three weeks, four weeks, or five weeks. Then they take it out and either wait a week or replace it with a new one. One NuvaRing has enough hormones in it to last for up to five weeks. It's 99 percent effective when used perfectly. The ring can be purchased through a pharmacy or health clinic with a

ESTROGEN AND HEALTH RISKS

According to Planned Parenthood, hormonal birth control methods are very safe. But some people with certain health problems might be at higher risk of a heart attack, blood clots, or stroke when using products that contain estrogen. Breast cancer patients, people who suffer from high blood pressure or serious migraines, and smokers over the age of 35 should not use the NuvaRing, the patch, the shot, or combination birth control pills.

prescription. It costs anywhere from zero dollars to $200, depending on health insurance.[10]

BIRTH CONTROL SHOTS

Similar to certain types of birth control pills, the birth control shot only contains the hormone progestin. It prevents pregnancy by stopping ovulation. Sometimes called Depo-Provera, the shot is administered by a doctor or other health-care provider every three months.

When used perfectly, this method is 99 percent effective. It costs anywhere from zero dollars to $150, depending on health insurance.[11] Two potential side effects of using the shot are a decrease in bone density and hair loss. In addition, women who are thinking about getting pregnant might have difficulty doing so for nine months after stopping this birth control method.

IUDs AND BIRTH CONTROL IMPLANTS

For people who want a lower-maintenance birth control option, birth control implants and IUDs are another choice. They mostly use hormones

The patch stops women from ovulating. This means there won't be an egg for a sperm to fertilize.

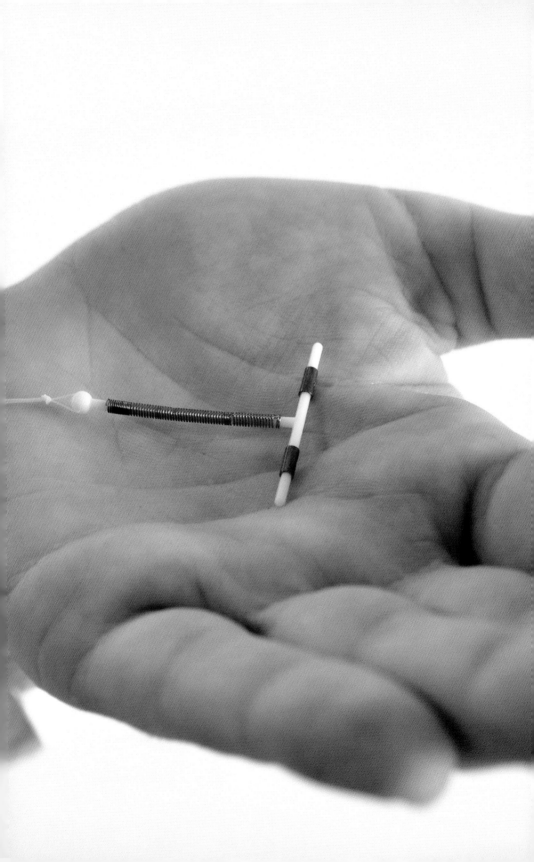

to prevent egg fertilization. Both are 99 percent effective and need to be inserted into the body by a physician. They can cost anywhere between zero dollars and $1,300, with removal costing between zero dollars and $300 depending on health insurance.[12] The implant looks like a small rod. It's inserted underneath the skin of the arm and uses progestin to prevent pregnancy for up to five years.

"THE IUD IS ONE OF THE MOST EFFECTIVE METHODS OF BIRTH CONTROL. IT TAKES OUT ALL OF THAT REMEMBERING. YOU CAN JUST FORGET ABOUT IT, AND YOU CAN FORGET ABOUT IT FOR YEARS."[13]

—MELISSA GILLIAM, ADOLESCENT GYNECOLOGIST AT THE UNIVERSITY OF CHICAGO

An IUD looks like a plastic T and is inserted into the uterus by a doctor. They are divided into two types. Copper IUDs have copper wire coiled around the device which triggers an inflammatory reaction that is toxic to sperm and eggs and blocks fertilization. They can prevent pregnancy for up to

IUDs are small, and there are various brands people can choose from.

STERILIZATION AND VASECTOMIES

Most forms of birth control are reversible. In most cases, once the birth control method is stopped the woman should be able to get pregnant. But there are also more permanent options. Sterilization is a surgical procedure that blocks a woman's fallopian tubes for good. It can cost thousands of dollars if not covered by health insurance. After the surgery, the woman might still have her period, but she can't have kids. A vasectomy is a similar procedure for men. The doctor cuts the man's vas deferens and ties them up so sperm can't leave the body. The procedure can cost up to $1,000 if not covered by health insurance.[14]

12 years. Hormonal IUDs use progestin to block ovulation. They can work for as long as three to seven years.

Both IUDs and birth control implants don't affect long-term fertility or make it harder to get pregnant in the future. While these methods might seem scary to use, they're low-risk and have minimal side effects, according to Planned Parenthood.

Finding the right birth control takes research, patience, and practice. What is right for one person might not be useful for another. When weighing the options, teens should consider the following questions: How easy will it be to get this method of birth control? Will a parent or guardian's consent be needed in order to purchase it? Is the choice affordable? Does it need to also protect against STIs? Does it involve hormones? Does it require keeping up with a schedule? Women can make an appointment with a doctor, counselor, or school nurse to discuss which form of birth control works best under their current circumstances.

"TO FEEL MORE IN CONTROL AND EMPOWERED ABOUT YOUR CONTRACEPTION CHOICES, THE FIRST STEP IS TO BE PREPARED. DO YOUR OWN RESEARCH BEFORE YOUR DOCTOR'S APPOINTMENTS, AND WRITE DOWN A LIST OF QUESTIONS."[15]

—DR. MARA GORDON, HOST OF NATIONAL PUBLIC RADIO'S LIFE KIT PODCAST

With the rates of teen pregnancy falling, more young people can keep their focus on schoolwork instead of raising a child.

CHAPTER FOUR

TEEN PREGNANCY ON THE DECLINE

In modern society, some teens are looked down upon for having kids too early. That wasn't always the case. Hundreds of years ago the average life expectancy was 35 to 40 years old. Women had babies at much younger ages than they do today. But as industrialization happened and women started working outside the home, many postponed having children until their twenties and thirties.

In addition to women delaying childbirth, the rates of teen pregnancy have declined since the early 1990s. The rate includes pregnancies that end in a live birth as well as those that end in abortion or miscarriage. In 2018 in the United States, the number of teen births for girls of all major races and ethnic groups, ages 15 to 19, was around 17 births per 1,000 girls. That was a 7 percent decrease since 2017 and a 72 percent decrease since the rate peaked in 1991.[1] Health experts are still debating the factors contributing to this decline. There are three major theories. One is the impact of the acquired

TEEN BIRTH RATES IN 2008 AND 2018[2]

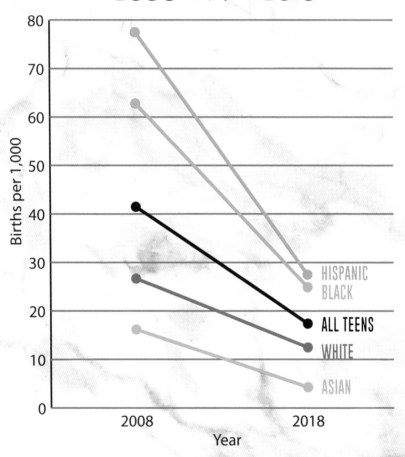

According to the Pew Research Center, in 2018 teen birth rates across many races and ethnicities were less than half of what they were in 2008. The chart shows birth rates per 1,000 girls ages 15 to 19.

immunodeficiency syndrome (AIDS) crisis and a resulting uptick in STI-preventative birth control use. Another is a shift in medical recommendations toward options such as implants and IUDs. The third is an increase in media exposure and access to sex education.

THE AIDS CRISIS

During the 1980s and early 1990s, a deadly virus was spreading rapidly across the United States and around the world, and it still exists today. Called the human immunodeficiency virus (HIV), it attacks and destroys cells in the immune system, inhibiting the body's ability to fight against disease. HIV is transmitted through bodily fluids such as semen, vaginal and anal fluids, and blood. It spreads through unprotected sex, blood transfusions, shared needles during drug use, and from mothers to babies during pregnancy, childbirth, or breastfeeding. If left untreated, the virus develops into a more serious illness called AIDS. People with AIDS are increasingly vulnerable to fatal infections, such as pneumonia and cancer.

According to the World Health Organization (WHO), more than 70 million people have been infected by HIV since the start of the HIV pandemic in the early 1980s. More than 35 million people have died of AIDS.[3] But doctors have made significant headway in fighting the disease. There are now medications that can help people who have

MAGIC'S ADMISSION

On November 7, 1991, Los Angeles Lakers basketball star Magic Johnson shocked the world when he went on television to reveal he had contracted HIV. At the time, the illness was believed to have been predominately spread by drug users and gay men. But Johnson revealed that he had gotten the disease by having unprotected sex with a woman.

Following his HIV diagnosis, Johnson made it his mission to educate people across the world about the virus and its effects. He started the Magic Johnson Foundation in order to address the educational, health, and social needs of ethnically diverse urban communities, especially teens. "Young people feel they're superman and superwoman and that nothing can ever happen to them," Johnson says. "So I felt it was necessary to get the word out to them . . . we have to worry about teen pregnancy, because that's also running rampant in our community unfortunately, and so many other diseases and viruses. HIV and AIDS is deadly."[4]

HIV live long and healthy lives. These medications can also stop the spread of HIV to other people. In fact, a 2019 study in the medical journal *Lancet* showed that antiviral treatments were instrumental in stopping the spread of HIV on a major scale over the last 40 years.

The increase in HIV-related scientific research and the rise in AIDS education programs throughout the 1980s and 1990s also had an unintended consequence. It persuaded more teens to wait longer before having sex and to use protection when they did have it. Thanks to outreach campaigns by public figures who were living with HIV, such as Los Angeles Lakers player Magic Johnson, AIDS activist Elizabeth Glaser, and teenage activist Ryan White, young people became so worried they'd contract HIV that they used condoms or had much less intercourse in general. Teens' use of condoms increased from 43 percent in 1991 to 63 percent in 2002. In 1996, the teen birth rate began a multi-decade decline that lasted through 2019 and beyond. "The teenagers of the 1990s were having less, and safer, sex—a nearly sure-fire recipe for fewer teens having babies," writes Sarah Kliff, senior policy correspondent at Vox.[5]

"[TEENS] HAVE TO UNDERSTAND THAT SOMETIMES YOU GOTTA BE BLUNT. . . . FIRST OF ALL, YOU HAVE TO MAKE THE RIGHT DECISION. BUT IF YOU MAKE THE DECISION TO HAVE SEX, YOU GOTTA TELL HIM, 'WE CAN'T DO NOTHING WITHOUT PROTECTION. DON'T EVEN THINK ABOUT IT.' AND THEN YOU MAKE HIM GO TO THE STORE."[6]

—*MAGIC JOHNSON, BASKETBALL PLAYER WITH HIV*

SHIFTING MEDICAL RECOMMENDATIONS

Another reason for the decline in teen pregnancy after 1991 was increased access to birth control options such as implants and IUDs. In the 1980s and 1990s, girls would

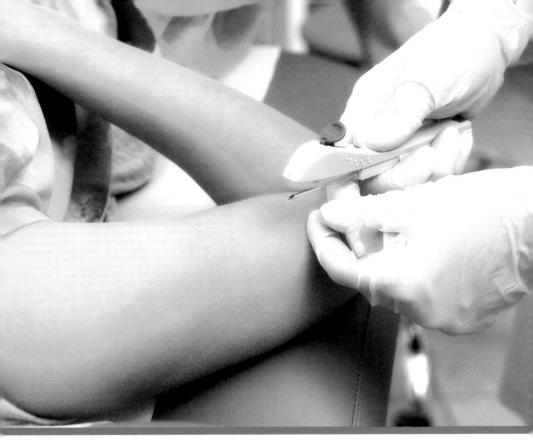

New policies in the 2000s made it easier to access hormonal birth control, including implants.

have to schedule a routine pelvic exam in order to be prescribed certain types of birth control. But in the early 2000s, medical groups such as the WHO, the American Cancer Society, and the American College of Obstetricians and Gynecologists (ACOG) updated their medical recommendations to make it easier for teens and women to access hormonal contraceptives without having to get a pelvic exam.

In 2005, the ACOG also issued Clinical Guideline 539. This recommendation stated for the first time that long-acting, reversible contraceptives such as implants and

IUDs should be the first line of contraceptives for all women, including teens. By 2013, 7.1 percent of US girls ages 15 to 19 were using these devices.[7] While that number is still small compared to condom usage, it could partially explain the decline in teen pregnancy. For example, between 2009 and 2013 the teen birth rate in Colorado dropped by 40 percent after a privately funded birth control program started giving free implants and IUDs to low-income teens.[8]

AN EXPERIMENT IN COLORADO

Between 2009 and 2013, the Colorado Family Planning Initiative provided thousands of birth control implants and IUDs to low-income girls and women for free. In addition to a 40 percent drop in the state's teen birth rate, there was also a 23 percent decrease in cases at Colorado WIC, a nutrition program for low-income mothers and their babies. "[The program] has helped thousands of young Colorado women continue their education, pursue their professional goals, and postpone pregnancy until they are ready to start a family," said Colorado governor John Hickenlooper in 2014.[9]

But the program did attract criticism. Some people said such easy access to contraception encouraged promiscuity. Others argued that because the clinic didn't require parental consent in order for a teen to receive birth control, the program interfered with a parent or guardian's role in raising their children.

MEDIA INFLUENCE AND SEX ED PROGRAMMING

A third possible contributing factor to the decrease in teen pregnancy after 1991 was the availability of sexual education for teens overall. Since the mid-1990s, an increase in federal, state, and locally sourced funding has made it possible for more pregnancy awareness programs that are specifically geared toward young people. For example, Power to Decide, formed in 1996, provides teens with up-to-date, research-based information on sexual health and contraceptive methods so they can make educated decisions about their futures.

In the early 2000s, internet usage skyrocketed, especially after the release of the

"ENSURING THAT ALL YOUNG PEOPLE HAVE THE POWER TO DECIDE IF, WHEN AND UNDER WHAT CIRCUMSTANCES TO GET PREGNANT, HELPS THEM ACHIEVE THE FUTURES THEY WANT. OVER THE PAST TWO DECADES, WE HAVE INVESTED IN ACCESS TO CONTRACEPTION AND QUALITY SEX EDUCATION. THESE PREVENTION PROGRAMS HAVE BEEN STRONG INVESTMENTS, AS THEY HAVE CONTRIBUTED TO EVER DECLINING TEEN PREGNANCY AND BIRTH RATES."[10]

—GINNY EHRLICH, CHIEF EXECUTIVE OFFICER OF POWER TO DECIDE

first iPhone in 2007. In 2018, the majority of teenagers had access to a smartphone. Unlike earlier generations, when teens had to rely on guidance from their parents or guardians, or from school-based sex education programs or counseling, the internet made access to sex education free, easy, and most importantly, anonymous. "Teenagers now have access to information they never had before; they can Google the sex questions that would have been far too embarrassing to ask any parent," writes Kliff. "That, in turn, could lead to teenagers becoming more educated about pregnancy risks."[11]

Messaging about sex and using birth control became more

MIND-CHANGING MESSAGING IN MILWAUKEE

In 2008, Milwaukee, Wisconsin, had the second-highest teen birth rate of any city, after Baltimore, Maryland. But the city's government boldly claimed it could reduce that rate by 46 percent by 2015. The city actually reached its goal two years early, eventually slashing the teen pregnancy rate by half.

The campaign succeeded partially because local businesses got in on the messaging. They released ads that showed shirtless teen boys with pregnant bellies and the tagline, "It shouldn't be any less disturbing when it's a girl."[12] Newspapers printed articles citing teen pregnancy statistics and tips on how to reduce risky behavior. The United Way of Greater Milwaukee also set up pregnancy prevention classes for at-risk teens.

With more access to education and contraceptives, teens can go through their lives without the stress of an unplanned pregnancy.

widespread and explicit in print media, movies, and television too. According to a scientific paper published in 2014, reality TV shows played a role in decreasing pregnancies. Shows that starred pregnant teens who struggled to stay in high school, maintain relationships, or hold down jobs after becoming pregnant contributed significantly to the decline in teen births during the shows' first 18 months on the air. University of Maryland economist Melissa Kearney and Wellesley College economics professor Phillip Levine, the study's authors, estimated the shows were responsible for a 5.7 percent decrease in teen births from 2009 to 2011.[13]

Whatever the reasons, the decline in teen birth rates since the 1990s has improved public health and poverty statistics. After all, teen mothers are more likely to drop out of high school, hindering their job prospects and ability to make or save money. What's more, children born to teen mothers are more likely to have lower earnings and become teen parents themselves. Though teen pregnancy can affect people of any race or cultural background, some races are more affected than others. Not only that, but access to pregnancy prevention and sex education programs varies widely across states and even within towns and urban areas. This can have far-reaching effects on not only individuals, but on society as a whole.

Pro-life and pro-choice advocates in the United States are very vocal about their beliefs.

CHAPTER FIVE

PUBLIC POLICY AND DEMOGRAPHICS

Many experts in sexual and reproductive health believe that all teens should have access to programs that give them the tools they need to approach sex with confidence while also preventing STIs and pregnancy. But across the United States, state governments and federal leadership have been divided about how to approach sex education and birth control services. For example, during the George W. Bush presidential administration between 2001 and 2009, federal and state governments spent more than $1.5 billion on education programs that pushed abstinence as the best way to control birth rates and the spread of STIs.

In the early years of the Barack Obama administration, which lasted from 2009 to 2017, Congress put $55 million toward abstinence-until-marriage programs. But it also allocated approximately $185 million for comprehensive sex education programs that provided teens with medically accurate and age-appropriate information about contraception, pregnancy, and HIV and STIs in case they did choose to have sex.[1] In 2010, the Obama administration created the Teen Pregnancy Prevention Program (TPPP), an initiative that gave funding to organizations working to find solutions to the teen pregnancy problem outside the abstinence-only approach.

When President Donald Trump took office in January 2017, his administration reversed a number of these policy issues. In 2018, the administration mandated that any recipient of TPPP funding would have to return to prioritizing abstinence-only sex education over all others. It would also have to emphasize that sex is a risky behavior that teens should avoid.

"RESEARCH SHOWS THAT ADOLESCENTS NEED MORE COMPREHENSIVE EDUCATION, NOT LESS, AND INCREASED ACCESS TO CONTRACEPTIVE SERVICES, NOT LESS. TO ARGUE ANYTHING ELSE MISSES AN OPPORTUNITY TO SUSTAIN THESE [DOWNWARD] TRENDS [IN TEEN PREGNANCY]."[2]

—HEATHER BOONSTRA, GUTTMACHER INSTITUTE

Opponents of Trump's policies saw these changes as a blow to all the progress made on curbing teen pregnancy during the previous three decades. "At the end of the day, the credit for the declines in teen pregnancy goes to adolescents themselves, who are making an effort to prevent unintended pregnancy," says Heather Boonstra of the research organization Guttmacher Institute. "The question now is whether society will do its part by adopting policies that support and equip young people with knowledge, skills, and services to stay healthy."[3]

GEOGRAPHICAL DIFFERENCES

In addition to differences at the federal level, the approach to sex education and whether teens have access to birth control varies across states. For example, Washington, DC, and 27 states, including California, New York, and Massachusetts, allow teens to access birth control services without parental consent. Teens can also access STI-related services in every state and in Washington, DC. But in 18 states, such

CHANGES IN POLICY

During the first three years of Trump's presidency, sex education policy took an abstinence-only approach. But on February 11, 2020, the president issued an announcement that future TPPP grant recipients would be able to focus on promoting teen health, including equal access to accurate and age-appropriate reproductive health options in order to reduce teen pregnancy.

Another development was the proposal of the Real Education for Healthy Youth Act. Submitted to Congress in 2019, it proposed redirecting funding for abstinence-only initiatives to programs that would teach young people about birth control options and how to have sex responsibly.

THE SUPREME COURT AND BIRTH CONTROL

In July 2020, the Supreme Court made a ruling that would affect birth control access. Under the Obama administration's Affordable Care Act, employers needed to cover birth control costs. However, certain religious organizations and companies could opt out of this requirement. The Trump administration tried to open this exemption up more and let additional employers opt out of covering birth control. The conflict over whether his administration could do this brought the case to the Supreme Court, which ruled in favor of the Trump administration's policy.

Writer Kate Baggaley at *Popular Science* notes, "The new decision . . . allows more employers to refuse to provide health insurance that covers the cost of contraception. Now virtually any employer . . . can seek an exemption from the Trump administration based on religious objections." Experts estimated the Court's ruling could leave between 70,500 and 126,400 people without access to birth control.[4]

as Alabama, Georgia, and Michigan, the doctor can also notify the parent if she or he deems it necessary.

After a teen gets pregnant, the laws surrounding what she can and cannot access without parental consent are different too. In most states, these rules apply to teens who have not yet become a legal adult. In North Dakota, people who aren't legal adults can get prenatal treatment during the first trimester of the pregnancy, but they must bring a parent or guardian along during the second and third trimesters. Five states, including Louisiana, Pennsylvania, and

Minnesota, require the consent or notification of a parent in order for an adoption to go through. Only two states—Connecticut and Maine—allow pregnant girls who are not legal adults to have an abortion without the consent of a guardian.

While these laws aren't the only reason why some states have a higher teen pregnancy birth rate than others, there is some correlation. For example, in 2018 the state with the lowest rate was Massachusetts, at 7.2 births per 1,000 females ages 15 to 19 according to the CDC. Alabama had a higher rate, at 25.2. New York and California

MASSACHUSETTS AND TEEN PREGNANCY

In 2018, Massachusetts had the lowest teen pregnancy rate in the United States. The state doesn't require schools to teach sex education; local school boards make that decision. But if there is a program in place, state standards mandate that the curriculum must include information about STIs and HIV/AIDS, teen pregnancy, family violence, birth control options, and inclusive ideas about sexual orientation.

Also, teens in Massachusetts don't need to notify a parent if they want to get tested for STIs or HIV/AIDS. They can also buy a pregnancy test, condoms, the morning-after pill, and other types of emergency contraception, and they can get a prescription for birth control. One thing teens are required to do in Massachusetts is get a guardian's permission to obtain an abortion. If the pregnant person's life is in danger or if the pregnancy is a result of rape or incest, the abortion is paid for by the state's Medicaid health insurance program.

Having and raising a child is difficult, but some young people decide to undertake that challenge.

had fairly low rates, at 11.7 percent and 13.6 percent respectively.[5]

SOCIOECONOMIC DIFFERENCES

Outside geographic differences, socioeconomic conditions within communities and families play a huge role in influencing the teen pregnancy rate. Girls from low-income, less educated families are more likely than their wealthier peers to become pregnant. For example, teens who are a part of the welfare system are at higher risk of teen pregnancy and birth than other groups. Girls living in foster care are more than twice as likely to become pregnant than those who don't live in foster homes. Other contributing factors include economic or racial disparity within neighborhoods, a high unemployment rate, and unequal access to high-performing schools and health care. "Among teens with lower socioeconomic status, there is a clear pattern of teen fertility across inequality categories," report Melissa Kearney and Phillip Levine. "Teens in the highest-inequality states are roughly 5 percentage points more likely to give birth as a teen than teens in the lowest-inequality states."[6]

Many local and national groups are working to combat the problem. Perhaps the most groundbreaking change happened in 1970 when the Supreme Court

> "WE BELIEVE THAT WITH IMPROVED ECONOMIC OPPORTUNITIES, REDUCED POVERTY, AND IMPROVED PROSPECTS FOR OTHER ADULT OUTCOMES, TEEN PREGNANCY [WILL] ALSO DECLINE."[7]
> —ECONOMISTS MELISSA KEARNEY AND PHILLIP LEVINE

ALL TOGETHER NOW

In 2015, the CDC's Division of Reproductive Health awarded hundreds of thousands of dollars to Sexual Health Initiative for Teens North Carolina (SHIFT NC), a Title X–funded organization in Durham, North Carolina. With the money, SHIFT NC created a five-year program called All Together Now. It worked with teens in foster care, juvenile detentions centers, and low-income public schools to get them greater access to birth control, sex education, and health-care services with the hope of reducing teen pregnancy and births in the long term.

According to the organization Power to Decide, in North Carolina there were 6,303 children born to girls ages 15 to 19 in 2018. That was a 73 percent decrease from the peak in 1991. Seventy-four percent of teen pregnancies occur in girls ages 18 to 19, and pregnancies in minors have become increasingly rare.[9] Many experts attribute the drop in teen pregnancies to increased access to contraception.

passed Title X. The law made it possible for people from low-income areas to access affordable birth control and reproductive health care, regardless of health insurance. In 2020, more than four million people were able to obtain an annual wellness exam, screening for breast and cervical cancer, testing and treatment for STIs and HIV/AIDS, and contraception thanks to Title X funding. According to Planned Parenthood, these types of publicly funded birth control services have prevented 1.9 million unintended pregnancies, including 440,000 teen pregnancies, every year.[8]

RACE AND TEEN PREGNANCY

Just as teen pregnancy affects lower socioeconomic groups the hardest in the United States, the rates are higher for some races than others. But all are on the decline. According to the CDC, in 2017 American Indian and Alaska Native teens ages 15 to 19 had the highest birth rate, at 32.9 births per 1,000 females. Hispanic teens and non-Hispanic Black teens had the second- and third-highest rates, at 28.9 and 27.5 respectively. Non-Hispanic white teens were next at 13.2. Asian teens were the lowest group at 3.3.[10]

A year later, those numbers dropped even more. In 2018, American Indians and Alaska Natives had the highest birth rate at 30 births per 1,000 females.[11] This was followed by 26.7 births for Hispanic girls. Non-Hispanic Black teens were next in line, with 26.3 births per 1,000 females, and non-Hispanic white teens were at 12.1.[12] Asians hovered at 3.[13] The discrepancy between races could be due to a number of contributing factors. Some health experts argue that Hispanic teens are less likely than teens of other races or backgrounds to either use contraception or talk to their partner about contraception before sex. Others suggest that many Hispanic teens and their families don't think of having a baby before age 20 as a negative thing.

Unplanned pregnancies also affect teen dads. Consequences for them include financial issues and lower educational achievement.

The age of the father and his access to birth control and appropriate reproductive health care information might play a role too. The earlier boys have sex, the less likely it is for them to know about birth control, have access to birth control, or opt to use birth control. According to studies conducted by the Guttmacher Institute, about one in four non-Hispanic Black males reported having sex before the age of 13 in some cities. For example, in Chicago, Illinois, the percentage of boys who had sex before age 13 was 29 percent among non-Hispanic Black males, 10 percent among non-Hispanic white males, and 11 percent among Hispanic boys. "Too often, the sexual health needs of young men are overlooked," says Guttmacher Institute researcher Laura Lindberg. "Outdated attitudes and harmful gender stereotypes leave many young men without needed information and services."[14]

Telling a partner about an unplanned pregnancy can be stressful, but it's an important conversation to have.

CHAPTER SIX

MAKING THE CHOICE

For most teens, finding out about an unplanned pregnancy is stressful. Figuring out what to do next might seem easy or totally insurmountable. There are three options: parenting, adoption, or abortion. Each one comes without guarantees. Each one has long-lasting consequences. Every situation is different. The only people who can decide what to do are the person who is pregnant and potentially her sexual partner.

Before making the decision, girls should confide in someone who is supportive. Friends are important, but leaning on a knowledgeable, reliable adult—someone with whom to discuss feelings and next steps—is vitally important. If girls can talk to a parent or guardian without fear of getting yelled at or judged, that's ideal. But sometimes that's not an option.

If talking to a parent or guardian isn't possible, there are other types of people to approach for accurate, nonjudgmental guidance. Some include a trusted nurse or counselor at school, a health-care professional or primary care physician, a social worker or therapist, or even an extended relative. There are also many national

> "IN MY SENIOR YEAR OF HIGH SCHOOL I BECAME PREGNANT. I WAS SCARED AND DIDN'T TELL MY PARENTS UNTIL WELL INTO MY FIRST TRIMESTER. DURING THAT TIME I RECEIVED NO REGULAR PRENATAL CARE, PUTTING THE HEALTH OF MY CHILD AT RISK. I WAS YOUNG, SCARED, AND ALONE."[2]
>
> —JACKIE CUMMINS, BLOGGER AT WHAT TO EXPECT

organizations with local chapters throughout the United States that staff certified therapists, counselors, and doctors who can advise pregnant teens. Planned Parenthood is one. The All-Options toll-free hotline (1-888-493-0092) is another. It's completely anonymous and open to people of all ages, genders, races, sexualities, backgrounds, religious affiliations, and political leanings in the United States and Canada.

Knowing which move is the "right" one will probably feel impossible. But weighing the pros and cons of each option is not only smart, it's necessary. Waiting too long without getting the proper care can cause harm to both the mother and fetus during pregnancy or cause complications during an abortion. "Teens who test positive for pregnancy should know their options and resources and act quickly," says Sarah Saxbe, an outreach coordinator for Nationwide Children's Hospital Teen and Pregnant Program.[1]

CHOOSING PARENTING

Choosing to parent is one option for pregnant teens. They might make this decision because having an abortion is against their religion or goes against the cultural values of their family. Other teens might choose to marry the baby's father or get engaged until the time is right to wed. Still others might rely on physical and financial support from parents or extended relatives to help raise the baby so they can stay in school or hold down a job in order to keep options open. Finishing high school or working long hours while raising a baby can be difficult. But assistance from family and friends can sometimes lighten the burden.

Many people who choose to become parents say it's the most joyful and rewarding decision they ever made. But having a baby is a lifelong commitment. There are

QUESTIONS TO ASK WHEN YOU'RE EXPECTING

Choosing whether to parent, place the baby for adoption, or have an abortion is one of the toughest choices a pregnant teen will have to make. There are some questions the teen can ask to help navigate the decision-making process, such as: How will the decision affect my future? Will it affect other family members? Am I ready to raise a child right now? Do I have the emotional support to raise a child as a teen? Is anyone pressuring me? Do I have religious or personal beliefs that would influence my choice? How will this decision affect my finances and job prospects?

Baby supplies aren't cheap, but sometimes people can find quality items at secondhand stores.

a few important things to know before taking on the responsibility. Raising a baby as a young person, either alone or with a partner, is time-consuming and energy draining, especially in the early years. It's also expensive, with an ongoing need for diapers, clothes, toys, and food.

There are health risks too. Pregnant teens have a greater risk of getting high blood pressure than pregnant women in their twenties or thirties. Pregnant teens also are more likely to suffer from preeclampsia. This is a dangerous medical condition that involves high blood pressure. It causes swelling in the hands and face, and it can possibly trigger organ damage. Preeclampsia can also cause complications in the pregnancy, including premature birth and miscarriage. Scheduling a prenatal appointment with a doctor right away is key. The doctor can prescribe vitamins for the mother and baby and help put together a pregnancy plan for the next nine months.

CHOOSING ADOPTION

There are many reasons why girls choose adoption over raising the baby on their own. They might not be ready to parent or can't afford to do so. Some girls may want to finish high school, go to college, or embark on a career before starting a family. Other girls might be in an abusive relationship or with someone they

PREMATURE BABIES

A full-term pregnancy lasts for 37 to 40 weeks. But some babies are born early. Any baby that is born before 37 weeks is considered premature. Sometimes a premature baby has to be delivered early in order to keep the baby and mother healthy. The earlier a baby is born, the more likely he or she is to suffer from respiratory, digestive, or cognitive problems.

Teens are at higher risk of having premature babies because of their biological immaturity and the fact that teenage mothers are more likely to be underweight than their older counterparts. Compared to full-term babies who weigh 7.6 pounds (3.4 kg) on average, premature babies can weigh as little as 3.3 pounds (1.5 kg). Babies born this small have to be put on a ventilator in a hospital. This medical device helps them breathe.

don't want to be connected to long-term. Whatever the situation, choosing adoption is a path toward a workable future. However, putting the baby in the care of someone else can be painful for a birth mother.

Adoption is a legal, binding, and permanent agreement that places a child in the care of another individual or family. There are two types. A closed adoption is confidential. That means the birth parents and adoptive parents have limited information about each other. While they might stay in touch during the adoption proceedings, they both agree to relinquish contact when the process is over. An open adoption is more flexible. The parents meet before the adoption begins, and they continue to stay in touch during the pregnancy and after the baby is born. The child is usually informed that he or she is adopted, and can stay in touch with both sets of parents depending on the terms of the adoption.

The adoption process is usually handled one of three ways. Independent adoptions happen between individuals with the help of an adoption

Adoption helps some couples or individuals who can't have a baby on their own.

lawyer. A kinship adoption is when someone from the biological parent's family assumes legal guardianship over the child, usually through a lawyer or the state department of human services. Many people use a third method: adoption agencies. These state-licensed organizations walk the biological parents through the process, including helping them screen and pick out suitable options for adoptive families. Some agencies even help with hospital arrangements and provide legal advice. The laws for adoption are different in every state, so it's important to do the research before making a decision.

THE NATIONAL PRO-CHOICE ADOPTION COLLABORATIVE

The National Pro-Choice Adoption Collaborative (NPCAC) is a national nonprofit organization. It is dedicated to providing accurate information about adoption to expecting mothers and their families. Though providing open adoption services is its main goal, it is also pro-choice, which means it discusses abortion as an option. NPCAC isn't religiously affiliated, and it accepts clients of all races, genders, and backgrounds, including people from the lesbian, gay, bisexual, transgender, and queer (LGBTQ) community. By 2020, NPCAC had placed thousands of children in adoptive homes. It has centers on the East and West coasts. It also has a 24-hour hotline.

CHOOSING ABORTION

Contemplating an abortion is tough, but it's not uncommon. Millions of people all over the world have had one. According to Planned Parenthood, about four in ten women who get pregnant decide to have an abortion each year in the United States. Overall, one in four women in the United States will have an abortion by the time they are 45. In addition, six out of ten people who get an abortion already have kids and want to focus on the children they have.[3] Other people who don't have children but have an abortion decide to have kids later on. Still other women don't want to have children at any point in their lives.

There are two types of abortions. Both are safe and effective. In-clinic abortions are done at a medical office or similar clinic such as Planned Parenthood. A trained doctor or nurse removes the pregnancy from the uterus using suction and a combination of surgical tools. The procedure takes about ten minutes and is successful

"REPRODUCTIVE JUSTICE IS BEING ABLE TO CONTROL AND DETERMINE FOR ONE'S BODY THE RIGHT TO PARENT OR NOT, THE RIGHT TO BEAR CHILDREN OR NOT, THE RIGHT TO ENGAGE IN SEXUAL BEHAVIOR OR NOT. THOSE DECISIONS ARE MADE WITH AUTONOMY AND FULL CONSIDERATION FOR THE PERSON BY THEMSELVES FOR THEMSELVES AS THEY SEE FIT."[4]
—MARIOTTA GARY-SMITH, COFOUNDER OF WOMEN OF COLOR SEXUAL HEALTH NETWORK

ABORTION RESTRICTIONS

Before deciding to have an abortion, it's important to research state laws. In 1973, the US Supreme Court case *Roe v. Wade* effectively made abortion legal in all 50 states. It recognized for the first time that the constitutional right to privacy "is broad enough to encompass a woman's decision whether or not to terminate her pregnancy."[5]

But ever since then, some states have made it much harder than others for abortion clinics to operate. For example, in July 2020, 43 states did not allow abortions after a certain point in the pregnancy, except if it was necessary to save the mother's life. Regarding pregnant teens, 37 states require some type of parental involvement in a minor's decision to have an abortion. Twenty-seven states say one or both parents must approve the procedure. Ten mandate that one or both parents of the teen must be notified if abortion is being considered as an option.

a vast majority of the time. Abortions after the first trimester often take longer and can be much riskier for the mother's health.

A medication abortion is one that uses two pills to end the pregnancy. This option is most effective when used during the first ten weeks of the pregnancy. The pills are prescribed by a doctor. Once a person takes the second pill, the uterus discards the pregnancy tissue through the vagina, much like what happens during a miscarriage. If taken within the first eight weeks of pregnancy, the pills are 94 to 98 percent effective. After 11 weeks, the method only works 87 percent of the time. Sometimes a third pill is prescribed to bring the effectiveness rate back up to 98 percent.[6]

PRO-CHOICE VS. PRO-LIFE

There is a lot of conflict in the United States over whether a woman should have the right to choose to have an abortion instead of having a baby. There are two major camps. People who are pro-choice believe that every person should decide when and whether to have children. Not all people who are pro-choice would make the decision to have an abortion if in the situation themselves, but they believe all women should have the option to do so in any circumstance.

People who are pro-life oppose abortion. Many believe life begins at conception. For them, having an abortion means murdering a child. "The pro-life message has been, for the last 40-something years, that the fetus . . . is a life, and it is a human life worthy of all the rights the rest of us have," said pro-life activist Ashley McGuire.[7]

People who are pregnant should plan out the financial costs of either keeping or giving up a baby.

CHAPTER SEVEN

THE COST OF PREGNANCY

When thinking about whether to have a child, it's important to weigh all the options. While money should never be the single deciding factor, it is one of the most far-reaching factors to consider. Delivering a baby, going through the adoption process, and getting an abortion each have different costs.

The least expensive option, at least for the pregnant teen, is adoption. While the laws are different in every state, adoption is usually low-cost or free for the biological mother. In most cases, the adoptive family pays for any reasonable pregnancy-related expenses that come up. That includes lawyer or adoption agency fees. Adoptive parents also pay for medical care not covered by health insurance or Medicaid, such as prenatal appointments, regular checkups with the obstetrician during the pregnancy, and delivery either at home or at the hospital.

Some adoption contracts require adoptive parents to pay for the birth mother's living expenses during the pregnancy too. For older women or teens living on their own, this might extend to rent and utilities.

> "I JUST WASN'T PREPARED TO BE A SINGLE PARENT AT THAT POINT IN MY LIFE. IT'S NOT SOMETHING MY FAMILY, OR SOCIETY, WOULD HAVE ACCEPTED AT THE TIME."[2]
>
> —JACQUI HUNT, WHO PLACED HER CHILD FOR ADOPTION WHEN SHE WAS 18

For younger teens, the stipend money could be used for maternity clothing, food, prenatal vitamins, transportation, and counseling.

But although this may sound like free money, getting reimbursed for pregnancy-related expenses is very different from getting paid to give birth. It's illegal to place a baby up for adoption in exchange for money. That's considered a form of child trafficking and has serious legal consequences, including jail time.

PAYING FOR AN ABORTION

For teens considering an abortion, the cost of the procedure depends on which method they choose, how far along they are in the pregnancy, and whether they have health insurance. It also varies by state. "Of all the complex factors that prevent women from accessing their constitutional right to an abortion, it seems like the price of the procedure should be one of the easiest things to understand," writes *Glamour* reporter Jennifer Gerson Uffalussy. "But even that can be tricky."[1]

Abortions that are done during the first trimester in a clinic can cost up to $1,500 without health insurance. If the procedure is performed later in the pregnancy, it's riskier for the woman's health and can be more expensive. Abortion surgeries performed in a hospital rather than a medical office are costlier too. For those who choose the abortion pill, it costs $504 on average without insurance.[3]

Some people aren't able to afford abortions—especially if they don't have insurance. In those cases, staff at Planned Parenthood may be able to help a person

PREGNANCY-RELATED EXPENSES?

According to the Child Welfare Information Gateway, it can cost tens of thousands of dollars to adopt a child in the United States. These figures include the cost of paying what the group calls reasonable pregnancy-related expenses for the birth mother. But what's considered reasonable?

There are different laws in every state to protect the people on both sides of the agreement. According to the Children's Bureau, seven states, including Illinois, Kentucky, and Minnesota, prohibit adoptive parents from paying for things such as educational expenses, a car, or vacations. Eighteen states also set a time limit for payments, ranging anywhere from 30 days to six months after the person gives birth. For example, Iowa allows the birth mother to obtain counseling for 60 days after the adoption, but it limits money for living expenses to 30 days.

find resources to bridge this financial gap.

THE PRICE OF RAISING A CHILD

In some developed countries, the price of delivering a baby is low. In Finland, for example, births cost less than the equivalent of $60.[4] But in the United States, unless the new mother-to-be is on Medicaid—in which case she will pay little to nothing to deliver a baby—she can expect to pay thousands of dollars even if she has private insurance.

As with most medical costs, childbirth prices vary by state and depend on the type of delivery. In New York City, for example, the cost of a vaginal delivery and post-hospital care in 2017 cost anywhere from $9,600 with insurance to $13,500 without. If the mother needed to have

Women can talk with a doctor to get more information about abortions.

a Cesarean delivery (C-section), the price went up. In Minneapolis-St. Paul, Minnesota, the cost was slightly lower. A vaginal delivery cost $4,200 with insurance and $7,600 without it.[6]

For after the baby is born, there are a number of purchases to consider that keep the newborn healthy and comfortable, including a car seat if the mother or father has a vehicle, a crib, a stroller, and clothes. Depending on the brand and whether these items are new or hand-me-downs, the cost could range anywhere from free to thousands of dollars. On top of those costs, there's the expense of diapers and nursing equipment or formula if breastfeeding isn't an option. Then, parents might have to add in day care expenses to the sum if a trusted family

COSTLY C-SECTIONS

A C-section is a procedure performed by doctors. They make cuts in the mother's abdomen in order to manually remove the baby from the mother's uterus. This type of surgery is usually performed if there are complications during the birth. Sometimes they are also scheduled if the mother doesn't want to go through vaginal delivery.

The cost of a C-section varies by state. The procedure is more expensive than a vaginal birth. In Colorado, the average cost of a C-section was around $10,000 with insurance and $17,500 without insurance. In Alaska, the average cost was approximately $16,700 with insurance and $28,600 without it.[7]

Day care can be expensive, but it also gives kids a good chance to socialize with others.

member or friend isn't available to help with childcare. Tack on post-pregnancy doctor visits for the mother and pediatric appointments for the baby, and the total cost for the first two years could reach tens of thousands of dollars.

As the child grows older, the costs keep going up. "New parents learn early on that everything costs much more than they anticipated," says Barbara Hetzer, author of *How Can I Ever Afford Children? Money Skills for New and Experienced Parents*. "And the expenses keep getting bigger as you go along."[8] For example, children and teens eat more than babies do. Their clothes are more expensive.

Between birth and age 18, some parents spend more than $200,000 on their child to cover shelter, food, and other necessities.[9] Some parents budget in additional money for their child's allowance, schooling and college education, and other extraneous expenses, such as entertainment or an extra car.

Teens shouldn't base their decision on whether to go through with the pregnancy solely on money. But it is a significant factor. The financial strain that comes with raising children could have a huge and long-lasting impact on their lives. Still, it isn't the only consideration. Having an abortion, placing the child up for adoption, or raising the baby can have a deep impact not only on teens' physical, emotional, and social lives, but on those of their support networks as well.

It's likely a person's financial plans for the future will have to be adjusted if he or she decides to have kids.

While not easy, parenting can have rewarding effects on a person's life.

CHAPTER EIGHT

EFFECTS ON DAILY LIFE

Being a teen is hard enough on its own. There are plenty of things to worry about—grades, crushes at school, getting along with parents or guardians, or insecurities. It can be a challenge just to develop into a cool, creative, and confident young adult. Add in an unplanned pregnancy and all the worry and planning that comes with it, and the word *challenge* becomes an understatement.

Aside from draining their finances, one of the biggest impacts unplanned pregnancies can have on teens is cutting their educations short. According to a 2018 report released by the nonprofit research organization Child Trends, only 53 percent of women in their twenties who became mothers when they were teens graduated from high school. About 17 percent earned the equivalent of a diploma by passing the GED test. In contrast, 90 percent of women who didn't get pregnant as a teen got a degree from high school.[1] Many of them went on to college and graduate school.

Being responsible for a child can make it difficult for a person to focus on schoolwork.

> "PARENTING IS SIMULTANEOUSLY WONDERFUL AND STRESSFUL AND CHANGES YOUR LIFE FOREVER."[2]
> —*SHANA LEBOWITZ, WRITER*

In addition, research from the CDC suggests that kids of teen moms are more likely to do poorly in school or drop out prematurely. They're also at greater risk of having health problems, being in jail at some point during their adolescence, being unemployed, and getting pregnant before they turn 20. Jennifer Manlove is a sociologist at Child Trends.

She notes, "We should maintain a focus on preventing teen births, but we also need to help improve the educational attainment of women once they become teen parents. Improving outcomes for young mothers can often improve outcomes for their children."[3]

PHYSICAL FALLOUT

Having a baby can be a wonderful event if all the right safety nets are in place. Many women—including teen moms—say their lives wouldn't be as fulfilling if they had opted to abort or go through adoption proceedings. But it's important to remember

STAYING HEALTHY

The body goes through many major adjustments during pregnancy. Breasts become tender and might go up a few cup sizes in preparation for making milk. Hormonal fluctuations can cause acne or the darkening of freckles. Other physical changes include leg swelling, constipation, backaches, and heartburn. In order for expecting mothers to keep their bodies healthy and strong, it's important to maintain a nutritious diet that includes plenty of fiber and vitamins, especially folic acid which helps prevent birth defects. Doctors recommend avoiding high-fat foods, alcohol, drugs, and smoking.

After giving birth, these same recommendations are key, especially if the mother is breastfeeding and passing on nutrients to her baby through the milk. "If you've decided to have a baby, the most important thing you can do is to take good care of yourself so you and your baby will be healthy," experts at Kids Health say. "Girls who get the proper care and make the right choices have a very good chance of having healthy babies."[4]

THE SILENT DOWNER

It's not uncommon for new mothers to feel a little sad after giving birth. The baby blues can affect many women—and even fathers—no matter their age. Teens are especially at risk, according to the CDC. This sadness can interfere not only with raising the child, but also with normal teenage emotional and physical development.

But there's also a more serious condition called postpartum depression. It usually starts one to two days after giving birth and can last for weeks, months, or up to a year after birth. Symptoms include constant crying, intense mood swings, extreme irritability, reduced concentration, lack of appetite, severe anxiety or panic attacks, and feelings of shame, guilt, or hopelessness. Sometimes people become suicidal. The Mayo Clinic recommends calling a doctor, seeking counseling, or contacting the National Suicide Prevention Lifeline (1-800-273-TALK; suicidepreventionlifeline.org/chat) if the symptoms last longer than two weeks, get worse over time, or become life-threatening.

that a baby isn't a doll, a pet, or a new friend. A baby is a living thing that requires constant, around-the-clock attention. A newborn relies on his or her parents for bathing, love, care, and food. A child can't be put away just because the mother or father is tired.

One of the hardest things about motherhood is its pace. Infants need constant attention, so there's very little time for sleep, especially in the first year. There might be many days when it isn't possible to take a shower, eat a nutritious meal, or get any sort of exercise. A woman of average weight before her pregnancy can

One abnormal side effect after an abortion is vomiting that lasts longer than 24 hours. If a person experiences this, she should check in with her doctor right away.

gain 25 to 35 pounds (11 to 16 kg) during pregnancy, so shedding pounds after the birth can be a challenge. It's not uncommon to feel exhausted, hungry, frustrated, and helpless all at the same time.

There are physical side effects involved with an abortion too. After the procedure, nausea is common. It can take a long time to heal. While it's possible to go back to school within the next day or two, cramping can occur. It's also normal for bleeding to continue for a week, if not more. But despite the discomfort, unless there's a rare and serious complication that goes untreated, there's no risk to a girl's overall health. It doesn't affect her fertility, and she can go on to have children in the future if she so chooses.

EMOTIONAL AND SOCIAL IMPACT

Teens faced with an unplanned pregnancy are likely to experience a vast range of emotions. Each girl's situation is different. Some might feel excited and overjoyed by the idea of giving birth, while others might suffer from intense anxiety or dread. "Teenagers who give birth are at greater risk for mental health concerns than older moms," says critical care nurse Rachel Nall. "But being aware of the risks and knowing where to find help can relieve some stress and pressure."[5]

Guilt is another common emotion that comes up. Some girls who decide to have an abortion or place the baby up for adoption feel confident about that choice and never look back. Others might feel relieved in the short term but regret it later on. For teens going through the adoption process, it can be especially nerve-racking. Choosing a suitable person or couple to parent the yet-to-be-born baby—and deciding whether the adoption should be open or closed—is difficult enough. But carrying the baby, then handing him or her over to someone else to raise, might trigger unexpected and powerful emotions that can take years to process. "I wish I could've found someone to help walk me through the process post-adoption," says a girl who chose to remain anonymous during an interview for *Cosmopolitan*. "I kind of lost my way for a while. I didn't cope with the pain I felt, so instead I fell into a steady stream of destructive behavior. I was punishing myself because I worried that my not being ready to be a mother had let [the baby] down."[6]

No matter which choice teens make,

CHOOSING YOUR PATH

In 2016, the *Atlantic* magazine published a series of firsthand accounts submitted by readers who had experienced an abortion. Many who wrote in had gotten pregnant as teens and decided to terminate the pregnancy. One letter-writer had gotten pregnant at 17. Her family life was a mess, and her boyfriend was controlling. When she found out she was pregnant, she immediately decided to have an abortion. Because she lived in Missouri, which required parental consent, she drove across the border to Illinois where the laws were looser.

"I had the abortion and didn't look back. I started making changes, and within two years I managed to extract myself," she wrote. "I moved away, went to college, got married, had a beautiful son on my own terms, went to grad school, and I've made this life into what I wanted. I wish everyone had that ability—to be in charge of their own life and destiny. To me there is no greater freedom than being able to choose your own future."[7]

emotional abuse or judgment from peers can be brutal during the pregnancy and afterward. Some girls lose their boyfriends, friends, and even their family's support once the news gets out. "I told my two 'best friends' that I was pregnant. One of them told her boyfriend who ended up telling his sister, and just like that, it spread everywhere. When I got back to school, the teachers looked down on me," recalls Kirstin Fitzgerald in an interview for *Teen Vogue*. "As for the rest of my friends, it was a scene from a movie: I got pregnant, and they ran away."[8]

If the stress of an unplanned pregnancy gets to be too much, seeking out a support network is essential to getting through the situation. Whether it is a parent or guardian, grandparent, guidance counselor at school, or health-care worker at a local clinic, finding someone to lean on who can help

> "THE BIGGEST PIECE OF ADVICE THAT I WOULD GIVE TO PEOPLE CONSIDERING ADOPTION WOULD BE TO WRITE DOWN WHAT YOUR EXPECTATIONS ARE AND HOW MUCH INVOLVEMENT YOU WANT TO HAVE WITH YOUR BIRTH CHILD AND THE ADOPTIVE FAMILY. THAT WAY, WHEN YOU ARE CONSIDERING POTENTIAL ADOPTIVE FAMILIES, YOU CAN COMPARE IT WITH THEIR EXPECTATIONS."[9]
>
> *—ANONYMOUS,* COSMOPOLITAN

Supportive friends can help teenagers get through the challenges of an unplanned pregnancy.

sort out the rollercoaster of thoughts and emotions can be extraordinarily helpful for the mind and body. While it might seem like the end of the world, getting through an unplanned pregnancy in one piece is not only possible but happens all the time.

ESSENTIAL FACTS

FACTS ABOUT UNPLANNED PREGNANCIES

- Any time a woman has vaginal sex and sperm are involved she can become pregnant. People who have vaginal sex without using any type of birth control have an 85 percent chance of getting pregnant within a year.

- Unplanned pregnancies affect teens of all racial, cultural, and socioeconomic backgrounds.

- There are many birth control options for sexually active people who don't want to get pregnant.

- Pregnant teens can choose to parent the child, give the child up for adoption, or get an abortion.

IMPACT ON DAILY LIFE

- Unplanned pregnancies can be very stressful for teens. It's important to seek help from a trusted adult in order to plan out the next steps.

- Pregnant teens must decide how they want to move forward with the pregnancy. Parenting, adoption, and abortion each have their own positive and negative aspects. Girls should try to think through all the benefits and consequences of their actions.

DEALING WITH UNPLANNED PREGNANCIES

- Pregnant teens can seek out help and support from family, friends, or medical professionals. They should think about the financial and emotional costs and benefits of having or not having a child.

- If a girl is going through with the pregnancy, she should schedule a prenatal appointment. The doctor can help come up with a pregnancy plan to keep mother and baby healthy.

- During and after pregnancy, a girl should maintain a nutritious diet that includes plenty of fiber and vitamins. Doctors recommend avoiding high-fat foods, alcohol, drugs, and smoking.

QUOTE

"Reproductive justice is being able to control and determine for one's body the right to parent or not, the right to bear children or not, the right to engage in sexual behavior or not."

—*Mariotta Gary-Smith, cofounder of Women of Color Sexual Health Network*

GLOSSARY

abstinence
The act of refraining from sex.

conception
The means of becoming pregnant, usually through fertilization.

contraception
Methods used to help prevent pregnancy.

infertility
An inability to become pregnant or to impregnate.

Medicaid
A health insurance program established in 1965 to assist children, pregnant women, and families as well as people with disabilities or blindness.

miscarriage
When a fetus dies in the womb before it has a chance to be born.

obstetrician

A doctor who specializes in pregnancy, delivery, the postpartum period, and the female reproductive system.

prenatal

Before birth, or relating to pregnancy.

pro-choice

Believing in a woman's right to choose whether she should have a baby or have an abortion.

pro-life

Believing that a fetus is a human child and should not be aborted.

puberty

The beginning of physical maturity when a person becomes capable of reproducing sexually.

trimester

In reproductive terms, one of three periods of approximately three months of pregnancy.

ADDITIONAL RESOURCES

SELECTED BIBLIOGRAPHY

Livingston, Gretchen, and Deja Thomas. "Why Is the Teen Birth Rate Falling?" *Pew Research Center*, 2 Aug. 2019, pewresearch.org. Accessed 29 June 2020.

Pardes, Bronwen. *Doing It Right: Making Smart, Safe, and Satisfying Choices about Sex.* Simon Pulse, 2013.

"Pregnancy." *Planned Parenthood*, n.d., plannedparenthood.org. Accessed 2 June 2020.

FURTHER READINGS

Akin, Jessica. *Pregnancy and Parenting: The Ultimate Teen Guide.* Rowman & Littlefield, 2016.

Ford, Jeanne Marie. *Understanding Reproductive Health.* Abdo, 2021.

Thiel, Kristin. *Dealing with Teen Pregnancy.* Cavendish Square, 2020.

ONLINE RESOURCES

Booklinks
NONFICTION NETWORK
FREE ONLINE NONFICTION RESOURCES

To learn more about unplanned pregnancies, please visit **abdobooklinks.com** or scan this QR code. These links are routinely monitored and updated to provide the most current information available.

MORE INFORMATION

For more information on this subject, contact or visit the following organizations:

Healthy Teen Network

1501 Saint Paul St., Ste. 114
Baltimore, MD 21202
410-685-0410
healthyteennetwork.org/teens-parents

The Healthy Teen Network provides up-to-date information and resources regarding sex, birth control, and reproductive health to adolescents and young adults, including those who are pregnant or parenting. It also offers counseling services to those in need.

Planned Parenthood Federation of America

123 William St.
New York, NY 10038
800-430-4907
plannedparenthood.org

Planned Parenthood provides accurate and current information about reproductive health care and sex education. It has more than 600 affiliated health clinics across the country with doctors and nurses that provide affordable care for many people.

SOURCE NOTES ▌

CHAPTER 1. A LIFE-CHANGING MOMENT

1. "Can You Get Pregnant the First Time You Have Sex?" *Planned Parenthood*, 14 Oct. 2010, plannedparenthood.org. Accessed 11 Aug. 2020.
2. Anna Medaris Miller. "5 Things to Know Before Taking an At-Home Pregnancy Test." *U.S. News*, 16 June 2015, health.usnews.com. Accessed 11 Aug. 2020.
3. "Teen Births." *CDC*, 27 Nov. 2019, cdc.gov. Accessed 11 Aug. 2020.

CHAPTER 2. GETTING PREGNANT AND THE SYMPTOMS

1. "Teen Pregnancy Issues and Challenges." *American Pregnancy Association*, n.d., americanpregnancy.com. Accessed 11 Aug. 2020.
2. Brittney McNamara. "How to Take a Pregnancy Test." *Teen Vogue*, 3 May 2019, teenvogue.com. Accessed 11 Aug. 2020.

CHAPTER 3. BIRTH CONTROL OPTIONS

1. "What Do I Need to Know About Birth Control?" *Planned Parenthood*, 2020, plannedparenthood.org. Accessed 11 Aug. 2020.
2. "Birth Control." *Planned Parenthood*, 2020, plannedparenthood.org. Accessed 11 Aug. 2020.
3. "Birth Control."
4. "Birth Control."
5. "Birth Control."
6. "How Effective Is Spermicide?" *Planned Parenthood*, 2020, plannedparenthood.org. Accessed 11 Aug. 2020.
7. "How Effective Is the Sponge?" *Planned Parenthood*, 2020, plannedparenthood.org. Accessed 11 Aug. 2020.
8. "Birth Control Pill." *Planned Parenthood*, 2020, plannedparenthood.org. Accessed 11 Aug. 2020.
9. "Birth Control Patch." *Planned Parenthood*, 2020, plannedparenthood.org. Accessed 11 Aug. 2020.
10. "Birth Control Ring." *Planned Parenthood*, 2020, plannedparenthood.org. Accessed 11 Aug. 2020.
11. "How Effective Is the Birth Control Shot?" *Planned Parenthood*, 2020, plannedparenthood.org. Accessed 11 Aug. 2020.
12. "Birth Control."
13. "A Guide to Navigating Birth Control." *NPR*, 20 Feb. 2020, npr.org. Accessed 11 Aug. 2020.

14. "Birth Control."
15. "A Guide to Navigating Birth Control."

CHAPTER 4. TEEN PREGNANCY ON THE DECLINE

1. "National Data." *Power to Decide*, 2020, powertodecide.org. Accessed 11 Aug. 2020.
2. Gretchen Livingston and Deja Thomas. "Why Is the Teen Birth Rate Falling?" *Pew Research Center*, 2 Aug. 2019, pewresearch.org. Accessed 11 Aug. 2020.
3. "History of AIDS." *History*, 30 Apr. 2020, history.com. Accessed 11 Aug. 2020.
4. Sarah Moughty. "20 Years After HIV Announcement, Magic Johnson Emphasizes: 'I Am Not Cured.'" *PBS*, 7 Nov. 2011, pbs.org. Accessed 11 Aug. 2020.
5. Sarah Kliff. "The Mystery of the Falling Teen Birth Rate." *Vox*, 21 Jan. 2015, vox.com. Accessed 11 Aug. 2020.
6. Moughty, "20 Years After HIV Announcement."
7. Livingston and Thomas, "Why Is the Teen Birth Rate Falling?"
8. Justin Caba. "Free Birth Control Initiative In Colorado Leads To A 40% Drop In Teen Birth Rates." *Medical Daily*, 9 July 2014, medicaldaily.com. Accessed 11 Aug. 2020.
9. German Lopez. "Colorado Offered Free Birth Control—and Teen Abortions Fell by 42 Percent." *Vox*, 7 July 2015, vox.com. Accessed 11 Aug. 2020.
10. "Declines in Teen Pregnancy and Childbearing Lead to Billions in Public Savings." *Power to Decide*, 31 Jan. 2018, powertodecide.org. Accessed 11 Aug. 2020.
11. Kliff, "The Mystery of the Falling Teen Birth Rate."
12. Kliff, "The Mystery of the Falling Teen Birth Rate."
13. Sarah Kliff. "6 Reasons Teen Births Are Plummeting." *Vox*, 29 May 2014, vox.com. Accessed 11 Aug. 2020.

CHAPTER 5. PUBLIC POLICY AND DEMOGRAPHICS

1. Heather D. Boonstra. "What Is Behind the Declines in Teen Pregnancy Rates?" *Guttmacher Institute*, 3 Sept. 2014, guttmacher.org. Accessed 11 Aug. 2020.
2. Boonstra, "What Is Behind the Declines in Teen Pregnancy Rates?"
3. Boonstra, "What Is Behind the Declines in Teen Pregnancy Rates?"

4. Kate Baggaley. "Supreme Court Ruling on Birth Control Could Have Ripple Effects Beyond Unwanted Pregnancy." *Popular Science*, 20 July 2020, popsci.com. Accessed 11 Aug. 2020.

5. "Teen Birth Rate by State." *CDC*, 28 Apr. 2020, cdc.gov. Accessed 11 Aug. 2020.

6. Stephanie Hanes. "Teenage Pregnancy." *Christian Science Monitor*, 22 May 2012, csmonitor.com. Accessed 11 Aug. 2020.

7. Hanes, "Teenage Pregnancy."

8. "Title X." *Planned Parenthood Action Fund*, 2020, plannedparenthoodaction.org. Accessed 11 Aug. 2020.

9. "North Carolina Data." *Power to Decide*, n.d., powertodecide.org. Accessed 30 Sept. 2020.

10. "About Teen Pregnancy." *CDC*, 1 Mar. 2019, cdc.gov. Accessed 11 Aug. 2020.

11. "National Data." *Power to Decide*, 2020, powertodecide.org. Accessed 11 Aug. 2020.

12. Joyce A. Martin et al. "Births in the United States, 2018." *CDC*, 24 July 2019, cdc.gov. Accessed 11 Aug. 2020.

13. "National Data."

14. "Young Men's Reports of Having Sex Before Age 13 Vary Widely by Their Race, Ethnicity and Geographic Area." *Guttmacher Institute*, 8 Apr. 2019, guttmacher.org. Accessed 11 Aug. 2020.

CHAPTER 6. MAKING THE CHOICE

1. "Risks of Teen Pregnancy." *Nationwide Children's*, 21 Oct. 2016, nationwidechildrens.org. Accessed 11 Aug. 2020.

2. Jackie Cummins. "Teenage Pregnancy Advice From a Mom Who's Been There." *What to Expect*, 29 Jan. 2015, whattoexpect.com. Accessed 11 Aug. 2020.

3. "Considering Abortion." *Planned Parenthood*, 2020, plannedparenthood.org. Accessed 11 Aug. 2020.

4. "A Guide to Navigating Birth Control." *NPR*, 20 Feb. 2020, npr.org. Accessed 11 Aug. 2020.

5. "*Roe v. Wade*." *Planned Parenthood*, Jan. 2014, plannedparenthood.org. Accessed 11 Aug. 2020.

6. "How Does the Abortion Pill Work?" *Planned Parenthood*, 2020, plannedparenthood.org. Accessed 11 Aug. 2020.

7. Emma Green. "Science Is Giving the Pro-Life Movement a Boost." *Atlantic*, 18 Jan. 2018, theatlantic.com. Accessed 11 Aug. 2020.

CHAPTER 7. THE COST OF PREGNANCY

1. Jennifer Gerson Uffalussy. "How Much Is an Abortion?" *Glamour*,
   23 Feb. 2020, glamour.com. Accessed 11 Aug. 2020.
2. David Dodge. "What I Spent to Adopt My Child." *New York Times*,
   18 Feb. 2020, nytimes.com. Accessed 11 Aug. 2020.
3. Uffalussy, "How Much Is an Abortion?"
4. Olga Khazan. "The High Cost of Having a Baby in America." *Atlantic*,
   6 Jan. 2020, theatlantic.com. Accessed 11 Aug. 2020.
5. Katie Adams. "Budgeting for a New Baby." *Investopedia*, 25 Jan. 2020,
   investopedia.com. Accessed 11 Aug. 2020.
6. "What It Costs to Have and Raise a Baby." *WebMD*, 2019, webmd.com.
   Accessed 11 Aug. 2020.
7. Hillary Hoffower and Taylor Borden. "How Much It Costs to Have a Baby
   in Every State." *Business Insider*, 9 Dec. 2019, businessinsider.com.
   Accessed 11 Aug. 2020.
8. Diane Harris. "The Cost of Raising a Baby." *Parenting*, 2020, parenting.com.
   Accessed 11 Aug. 2020.
9. Mark Lino. "The Cost of Raising a Child." *USDA*, 18 Feb. 2020, usda.gov.
   Accessed 11 Aug. 2020.

CHAPTER 8. EFFECTS ON DAILY LIFE

1. "Fewer Teen Moms but Still a Dropout Puzzle for Schools." *U.S. News*,
   22 Jan. 2018, usnews.com. Accessed 11 Aug. 2020.
2. Shana Lebowitz. "13 Hard Truths About Parenting No One Wants to
   Believe." *Business Insider*, 13 Feb. 2018, businessinsider.com. Accessed
   11 Aug. 2020.
3. "Fewer Teen Moms but Still a Dropout Puzzle for Schools."
4. "Having a Healthy Pregnancy." *TeensHealth*, Feb. 2017, kidshealth.org.
   Accessed 11 Aug. 2020.
5. Rachel Nall. "What Are the Effects of Teenage Pregnancy?" *Healthline*,
   19 Sept. 2019, healthline.com. Accessed 11 Aug. 2020.
6. Lane Moore. "What It's Really Like to Place Your Baby for Adoption."
   Cosmopolitan, 1 Feb. 2016, cosmopolitan.com. Accessed 11 Aug. 2020.
7. Chris Bodenner. "Getting an Abortion as a Young Teenager." *Atlantic*,
   11 Feb. 2016, theatlantic.com. Accessed 11 Aug. 2020.
8. Kirstin Fitzgerald. "Pregnant at Prom: My Life as a Teen Mom." *Teen Vogue*,
   6 May 2015, teenvogue.com. Accessed 11 Aug. 2020.
9. Moore, "What It's Really Like to Place Your Baby for Adoption."

INDEX

abortion, 11, 14, 45, 61, 69–71, 76–79, 81–83, 88, 93, 95–97
abstinence, 31, 57–59
abusive relationships, 73
acquired immunodeficiency syndrome (AIDS), 47–49, 61, 64
adoption, 11, 14, 59, 61, 69, 71, 73, 75–76, 81–83, 88, 93, 96–98
American Cancer Society, 50
American College of Obstetricians and Gynecologists (ACOG), 50
American Pregnancy Association, 18
anorexia, 22

birth control, 6, 13, 29–43, 47, 49–51, 53, 57, 59–61, 64, 66
birth control shot, 13, 29, 37, 39
bloating, 22
Bush, George W., 57

Centers for Disease Control and Prevention (CDC), 13, 61, 64–65, 92, 94
Cesarean delivery (C-section), 86
condoms, 6–7, 13, 17, 29, 31–32, 34, 49, 51, 61
cramps, 7, 23, 29, 35, 96
counselors, 14, 43, 69–70, 98

diet, 22, 93
drug store, 7–9

embryo, 21

female reproductive system, 19–21
    eggs, 6, 13, 19, 21, 23, 25, 29, 32, 34, 36, 41
    fallopian tubes, 19, 21, 42
    ovaries, 6, 19, 23
    uterus, 11, 19, 21, 34, 41, 77–78, 86
    vagina, 6, 19, 21, 24, 29, 32–34, 37, 78, 85–86
fertilization, 13, 19, 21, 25, 29, 41
fetus, 11, 21, 70, 79
folic acid, 93
foster care, 63–64

GED test, 91
Guttmacher Institute, 58–59, 66–67

health insurance, 35, 37, 39, 41–42, 60–61, 64, 81–83, 85–86
hormones, 8, 25, 29, 32, 35–37, 39, 42
    estrogen, 36–37
    human chorionic gonadotropin (HCG), 8, 25
    progestin, 36–37, 41–42
human immunodeficiency virus (HIV), 47–49, 58, 61, 64

implantation, 13, 23
infertility, 8
internet, 52–53
intrauterine devices (IUDs), 13, 39, 41–42, 47, 49, 51

Johnson, Magic, 48–49
judgment, 69, 98

male reproductive system, 18
   epididymis, 18
   penis, 18, 21, 32
   prostate gland, 18
   seminal vesicles, 18
   vas deferens, 18, 42
marriage, 57
Mayo Clinic, 31, 94
menstrual cycle, 19, 22–23, 25, 31
   irregular, 22–23, 25, 31
mental health, 13, 96
miscarriage, 45, 73, 78

nausea, 22, 35, 95
newborns and infants, 86, 94

Obama, Barack, 57–58, 60
ovulation, 19, 22–23, 29–31, 36–37, 39, 42

parental consent, 51, 59–60, 97
parenting, 14, 69, 71–73, 92
patches, 13, 29, 31, 36–37
pelvic exams, 50
period, 6–7, 9, 19, 22–23, 25–26, 35, 42
Planned Parenthood, 6, 10, 25, 29, 32, 34, 37, 42, 64, 70, 77, 83
postpartum depression, 94
Power to Decide, 52
preeclampsia, 72–73
pregnancy costs, 81–88
pregnancy test, 8–10, 13, 24–26, 61
premature birth, 73
prenatal appointments, 11, 73, 81
pull-out method, 6, 30

reality TV, 54
Roe v. Wade, 78

sex education, 47, 52–53, 55, 57–59, 61, 64
sexually transmitted infections (STIs), 30, 32, 34, 42, 47, 57–59, 61, 64
sperm, 13, 18–19, 21, 29, 32, 34, 36, 41–42
spotting, 23, 35
sterilization, 42
Supreme Court, 60, 63, 78

teen birth rates, 12, 46, 49, 51, 53, 55
Teen Pregnancy Prevention Program (TPPP), 58–59
Title X, 64
Trump, Donald, 58–60

United Kingdom, 12
unprotected sex, 6, 17, 31, 47–48
urinary tract infections, 34

vaginal rings, 13, 29, 37

World Health Organization (WHO), 47, 50

ABOUT THE AUTHOR

ALEXIS BURLING

Alexis Burling has written dozens of articles and books for young readers on a variety of topics including current events, famous people, nutrition and fitness, careers, money management, relationships, and cooking. She is also a book critic with reviews of both adult and young adult books. She has had articles published in the *New York Times*, *Washington Post*, *San Francisco Chronicle*, and more. Burling lives with her husband in Portland, Oregon.

ABOUT THE CONSULTANT

LAURA WIDMAN, PhD

Laura Widman, PhD, is a licensed clinical psychologist and an associate professor of psychology at North Carolina State University. She completed her PhD from the University of Tennessee and a postdoctoral fellowship in HIV/STD prevention at the University of North Carolina at Chapel Hill. Dr. Widman's research is focused on adolescent sexual communication and the use of technology-based interventions to improve sexual health among vulnerable populations.